T0354694

# SEASONS

## *Yesterday, Today and all those Tomorrows*

MARIE BISHOP

WESTBOW
PRESS®
A DIVISION OF THOMAS NELSON
& ZONDERVAN

WestBow Press books may be ordered through booksellers or by contacting:

WestBow Press
A Division of Thomas Nelson & Zondervan
1663 Liberty Drive
Bloomington, IN 47403
www.westbowpress.com
844-714-3454

ISBN: 978-1-6642-7438-9 (sc)
ISBN: 978-1-6642-7439-6 (e)

Library of Congress Control Number: 2022914117

Print information available on the last page.

WestBow Press rev. date: 01/17/2023

*The length of our days is seventy years,*
*eighty if we have strength!*
　　　　　　　　　　**—Psalms 90:10 (NIV)**

# CONTENTS

The Story behind the Story     ix

## SPRING

Chapter 1    A Time to Be Born     1
Chapter 2    A Time to Embrace     11
Chapter 3    A Time to Tear Down     19
Chapter 4    A Time to Rebuild     28
Chapter 5    A Time to Search     34
Chapter 6    A Time to Keep     42

## SUMMER

Chapter 7    A Time to Dream     53
Chapter 8    A Time to Laugh     61
Chapter 9    A Time to Love     70
Chapter 10    A Time for Even More Loving     78
Chapter 11    A Time to Embrace Change     84
Chapter 12    A Time to Laugh and a Time to Weep     91
Chapter 13    A Time to Die     100
Chapter 14    A Time to Be Born Again—with New Visions     108
Chapter 15    A Time to Tear—and to Mend     116
Chapter 16    A Time to Plant     121

## AUTUMN

| Chapter 17 | A Time to Accept New Experiences | 131 |
| Chapter 18 | A Time for Gathering | 138 |
| Chapter 19 | A Time to Heal | 147 |
| Chapter 20 | A Time to Speak | 157 |
| Chapter 21 | A Time to Rejoice | 166 |
| Chapter 22 | A Time to Mourn | 177 |
| Chapter 23 | A Time to Let Go | 188 |
| Chapter 24 | A Time to Dance | 192 |
| Chapter 25 | A Time to Scatter | 203 |
| Chapter 26 | A Time for Reconnaissance | 212 |

## WINTER

| Chapter 27 | A Time to Pull up Roots | 225 |
| Chapter 28 | A Time to Transplant | 230 |
| Chapter 29 | A Time to Mourn Brian, 1936–2007 | 236 |
| Chapter 30 | A Time to Mend | 245 |
| Chapter 31 | A Time to Throw Away ... Bad Attitudes | 253 |
| Chapter 32 | A Time to Tear Down and a Time to Rebuild | 260 |
| Chapter 33 | A Time to Live Till I Die | 265 |
| Epilogue | | 273 |
| About the Author | | 279 |

# THE STORY BEHIND
# THE STORY

**Turning seventy was my wake-up call!**

How did I get here so quickly? What have I done with all those years? How much time is left?

Did everyone have those thoughts or was God speaking to me, challenging me?

My family planned a wingding of a party to celebrate my three score and ten, with line dancing to Beatles music and '60s dress! Perhaps it was the music and clothes that took me back in time, triggering memories, igniting a desire to "write my memoirs", to share all those memories that would disappear with me when I popped my clogs.

There had been times when I'd recounted an event in my life, and the response was, "You should write a book!" Seriously?

My parents didn't reach seventy; they died at sixty and sixty-one, many of their memories going with them, unshared. Including my mother's Christmas cake recipe!

Shortly after my seventieth birthday, I made a start on my story. Initially, the intended audience was my children and grandchildren, and other family members and friends. But as "my story" unfolded, I wondered. Would it have wider appeal? Would it resonate with people who don't know me? Would they be encouraged by seeing the different outcomes in my life when God was at the helm. Would my experiences help others to see God's hand in their lives? Would it challenge them to write their story too?

As I pondered this, Pastor Mike preached on telling our story:

"Let the redeemed of the Lord tell their story" (Psalms 107:2, NIV).

The redeemed of the Lord! That's me! Does the command in Psalm 107 apply to *all* of God's children? Other scriptures told me yes: "Tell it to your children, and let your children tell it to their children, and their children to the next generation" (Joel 1:3, NIV).

My life has not been spectacular—no momentous achievements, nothing to write about really, unless it's recognising where God has been at work. So, I need to record, for my family and others, where He has answered prayers and directed paths, times when He has orchestrated events and changes in my life. Sometimes these events look like chance happenings, coincidences. But there have been others that could only be miracles. I can see them now as road markers, stepping stones as God guided me on my journey, not *co*incidences but *God*-incidences.

Catherine Marshall's book *Meeting God at Every Turn* impacted me thirty years ago. She recorded chapters of her life, the challenges, the victories, and the recognition of God's hand in each situation. Reading this book made me realise that God has always had His hand on me, too. He has answered my prayers—spoken or thought. He has met me at pivotal times in my life, guided me, and protected me. Even when I was wallowing in the mire of my mistakes, He was there. At the time I didn't always feel His presence or see His hand. But now, I can clearly identify those moments. Hindsight is a wonderful gift! God has, indeed, met me at every turn, just like Catherine Marshall's story.

Each season of my life has had its own climate—growth in different ways in each season, different challenges, and different countries.

My spring years were spent in war-ravaged Liverpool, England. My large loving extended family was my security.

Summer blossomed with immigration to Rhodesia—with romance, marriage, and children.

And then on toward then end of summer, Rhodesia became Zimbabwe—taking me through to my autumn years. This was a season of spiritual growth and recognising God's healing power.

Late autumn saw New Zealand become my home, and I am still here in the winter of my years. Even in winter there are crossovers. Spring pops up. New visions beckon! Is life on earth a training ground for eternity—a sort of seventy or eighty-year apprenticeship?

As I review what I have written, my early years, spring, seem somewhat passive compared with summer, which burst forth, long and loud, blossoming with new learning experiences. Then those years eased into the calm of autumn, a time of reassessment, before relaxing into winter for evaluation. My temptation was to prune the loud, lively summer, but then a vital point would be missed. Life is a *journey*—a succession of pathways as God guides us through each stage, teaching eternal truths. Growth through the seasons of life is God's design. There are markers, stepping stones on the journey.

When my winter years come to an end, a new journey will begin.

Years have passed since those first stirrings to write my story. My journal records my prayer: "Lord, please help me to get this done! I don't want to be a failure and leave my book half finished."

It is well under way but still a work in progress. After praying this prayer, I opened my daily reading booklet. The Word for that Day "happened" to be headed "When You Have A Vision"!

The first paragraph, so encouraging, read, "The vision is for an appointed time … though it tarries, wait for it, because I will surely come" (Habakkuk 2:3, KJV).

Maybe I am not such a failure, after all.

Maybe it's just a timing thing.

Maybe the time is *now*; my story *is* slowly taking shape.

I have a habit that can be annoying—a single word can trigger a song. Someone will say, "See you on Monday," and I will start singing "Monday, Monday!"

As I focus on writing this book, a song from my youth resurges. I don't know where it came from but find myself humming the tune, substituting my own words:

Someday I'm gonna write, the story of my life
The ups, the downs, laughter, and tears
Even in those wilderness years
When You guided me

(Verse 2)

I want the world to know, the story of my life
The moment I said the sinner's prayer
I knew you had been always there
And You became Lord to me

(Bridge)

The sorrow when I turned away from you
The memory of a grieving heart
The wonder as you drew me back to you
Never, never more to part.
There's one thing left to do, before my story's through
To tell the world of your guiding light,
So that the story of my life
Can start, and end, with You.

My life has not ended yet, but it did start out with God.
And I believe my hand will be in His when it does end.
So, where to begin? At the beginning seems a good place.

# SPRING

# ONE

# A Time to Be Born

World War II was declared six weeks after I arrived on this earth.

My parents, Les and Betty, had been married for a year when they welcomed their first child. Their home was a cute little cottage in Oddfellows Yard, Woolton, close to St. James Church, where Betty and her sister Nance, were members. That was where they presented me to be christened—claimed me for Jesus at two weeks of age! Nance, Nana to me, was my godmother. They made vows on my behalf, promising to raise me in the knowledge and love of God. And they did!

This was not unusual in 1939. But sadly, it's not the norm now. Parents have "naming days" instead of dedicating their children to Jesus and asking for God's blessing on their children's lives. I am so grateful I was blessed and dedicated from the get-go! Those vows made by my parents and godparents were repeated when I was baptised at fifteen and again at confirmation, when I joined the Anglican Church.

I don't recall Nannie and Granddad Findlay being members of a church, but Nannie loved to listen to church services on the radio and would sing along with the hymns, so she had some faith. They commissioned a beautiful shawl for my christening, embroidered and deeply fringed. This has also been used for both of my brothers, several cousins, friends, and my own children and grandchildren. It is now stored away waiting for the next generation.

My mother and godmother were both women of strong faith. Their mother, Gran Parker (née Maria Jones), came from a chapel upbringing in Wales. She was a down-to-earth Christian and worshipped at whichever church was nearest! Her Bible was in Welsh, and she often sang hymns around the house in her mother tongue. She was a strong character, red haired with a fiery personality! I was blessed to have a grandmother, a mother, and a godmother who were strong women with a down-to-earth faith in Jesus Christ, and I know they prayed for me from day one.

## Survival

On Sunday, September 3, my parents, together with the rest of Britain, tuned into the radio at 11 a.m. to hear Neville Chamberlain make the expected announcement. It was no longer "peace in our time"—England was at war with Germany. Betty and Les knew their lives were about to change.

The British government had been making evacuation plans for several months, fearing aerial bombardment of cities and towns, as witnessed during the Spanish Civil War. In September 1940, Operation Pied Piper began, evacuating the vulnerable away from cities. Children from Liverpool were transported to Cheshire or Wales into safer homes. The nation held its breath nightly, waiting to hear the drone of bombers. But nothing happened for almost a year. Many children were brought back home during this time of the Phoney War, despite the government's instructions to keep them away from cities.

By March 1940, there was a sense of urgency around the provision of bomb shelters. Anderson shelters, for single families, were installed in individual gardens, partially dug into the ground. Brick or concrete shelters were constructed in the middle of streets of terraced houses. These were large enough to accommodate several families. My parent's cute little cottage in Oddfellows Yard had become too small when they were expecting their second child. They moved to a two-bedroom terraced house in Tudwall Street, near Garston Gas Works, with three large air raid shelters down the middle of the street.

The bombing raids started in August 1940, accelerating over the following months into the Blitz. Liverpool was the second most bombed city in England. Night after night, there was intense, heartbreaking destruction. Many died, and many others became homeless; every family was affected in some way.

Children went to bed in siren suits, which were like today's onesies but made of thicker material and with a trapdoor in the back for toileting! When the air raid sirens screamed, mothers would grab their children and run to the shelters. They would all hunker down until the all-clear sounded. The men were active at nights with the Home Guard putting out fires and rescuing people from the rubble of bombed buildings. Les Findlay, although of call-up age, was in reserved employment and ineligible for enlistment initially, so he became part of the Home Guard. Liverpool was pounded nightly.

During autumn 1940, there was an outbreak of bronchial pneumonia. Seven children in our air raid shelter contracted the disease. There were no antibiotics available in 1940. My mother was heavily pregnant with Tony at the time; she told me how she prayed as she sponged and cared for her fourteen-month-old daughter. She kept vigil, night and day, waiting for the fever to break, overwhelmed by fear and heartbreak as, one by one, the other children died—five in all. Only Phyllis and I survived. God heard the prayers, the cries from the hearts of my family; it was the first miracle in my life.

My early childhood was a miracle of survival. Memories of that time are really my mother's shared memories. Thanks to my family, I carried no fear or anxiety, although surrounded by mounds of rubble from bombed buildings, some of which remained into my teen years. And despite stringent food rationing, I never recall feeling deprived or poor. There was always food on the table and warm clothes in winter. Betty had the wisdom to use and reuse whatever was in her hand, meeting all our family's needs. I believe that wisdom could only come from our loving Heavenly Father.

## Heroes

One terrifying event happened in the early hours of 29 November, 1940. A parachute bomb landed in the gas storage tank at the end of our street. It lodged inside the tank but did not explode. Police evacuated Tudwall Street and surrounds—thousands of people! The pram was loaded up with Tony and me and whatever else could be piled on top. The family headed out of the danger zone, part walking fast, part running the three kilometres to Nannie and Grandad's home in Meredith Place.

All good, until Tony's feeding time. His bottle had been left behind! Dad had to go back again to the now deserted street. The police allowed him to enter the house. He crept up the stairs engulfed in an uncanny silence. The feeding bottle had just been retrieved from their bedside table when a lorry backfired. His reflex reaction was to jump down the twenty-one stairs and race down the street, bottle in hand and away from impending doom.

The bomb was diffused by the heroic actions of Lieutenant Harold Newgrass, a veteran of World War I. He climbed inside the gas tank using a succession of oxygen masks, which only worked for a short time. The masks needed to be changed every thirty minutes. The selfless actions of that man, along with all the firemen, police, electricians, and plumbers saved the lives of us all. They were true heroes.

## Family Support

Despite the nightly bombings, all the houses we lived in survived unscathed! In 1941, the family moved into a slightly larger house in Earp Street, away from the Gas Works zone in Tudwall Street. This was to be our home for thirteen years. We lived on the Protestant side of the street next to the Baptist church and opposite St. Francis's Church on the Catholic side of the street. Liverpool is not nicknamed "the capital of Ireland" for nothing!

My father's reserved employment was with an iron foundry. Iron railings around houses were removed for smelting and reused as arms and ammunition. As the national need for iron diminished, those in reserved employment were called up for army service. Les Findlay's papers arrived early in 1944, and he started his army training assigned to the Royal Army Service Corp. Their battalion was shipped out to India on a troop carrier a month after Stuart was born, returning in 1948. Although Les Findlay experienced little of the war between Hitler and the rest of the Europe, he returned home four years later radically changed and deeply scarred by all he did experience while serving in India in 1945 to 1946 and in Japan in 1947.

Back in Garston, Betty somehow kept her three children fed and happy. Rationed food was minimal—the basics with no frills. Feeding the family must have been a challenge, but there were even cakes made with powdered egg, powdered milk, and no sugar—only saccharine—somehow combined into a delicious treat! At times, we shared our home with people who had been bombed out. This is where my own memories start. I remember Mrs Collier living in our front sitting room with her daughter, Moira, a girl my own age of four or five. Mr Collier was fighting the war, and their home had been reduced to a pile of rubble. A quiet young boy called Arthur shared Tony's bedroom for months. Where were his parents?

Our extended family was supportive. Nannie Findlay called in most evenings on her bicycle to check that we were okay. No phones in our homes back then. She cycled between Speke and the city each day to work in a large department store, seven miles each way at over sixty years of age. Her first stop was Aigburth to check on Auntie Nan and my cousins Pat and Ian and then on to our house in Garston before heading home. Then she would do it all again the next day! If the air raid siren sounded as she cycled, she would head into the nearest shelter, wait for the all-clear, and then carry on. Granddad Findlay was officially retired but worked sculling sailors out to ships anchored in the Mersey River basin.

Nana and Uncle Tom also lived in Garston. Uncle Tom worked on the docks in Garston, unloading the cargo from ships that had braved Hitler's submarines and U-boats in crossing the Atlantic Ocean. He shared his gleanings of damaged banana hands with the family. Nana was a tower of strength to her sister, my mum, helping her with the three children. Her own son Tony was serving in North Africa. Christmas and birthday gifts were usually revamped or home-made. Nana knitted garments and dolls' clothes using the wool unravelled from discarded jerseys.

## Anchor

The Baptist Church next door to our home in Garston was our anchor. We attended worship service each Sunday morning and Sunday school in the afternoon. I learned the joy of singing in a choir. When I was chosen to sing solo at the Children's Anniversary Service, the whole family was excited. But what to wear? The war was over, but England was still picking up the pieces. Both food and clothing were still rationed; there were no coupons to spare for frivolous new dresses. I had some nice hand-me-downs from my cousin Jean.

On anniversary morning, I came downstairs to a wonderful surprise. My darling mum had sacrificed her glamorous nightgown—Dad's gift sent to her from Japan. She'd sewn late into the night fashioning a new dress out of the pink satin, decorating it with lace roses at the neck and hemline cut from the family Christening veil. Christening veils were no longer in fashion, kept in drawers as heirlooms. Practical Betty saw the need was now and met it. I felt like a princess as I stood in front of the congregation singing, "It's the children's anniversary, long awaited day of joy …"

That time of clothes rationing also stimulated innovation, when latent and new skills surfaced. From the age of four, I attended dancing lessons with local teacher, Evelyn Rosen. Costumes for dance concerts taxed the initiative and were often fashioned from bleached and dyed flour sacks, bought cheaply from the local flour mill on the corner of Earp Street.

My first "ballet shoes" were homemade from double thickness flour sack material! There was a plentiful supply of discarded blackout curtain material as the war ended, waiting to be jazzed up with coloured rickrack or bias binding. Worn men's trousers were prized to make into small pants for small boys.

When Dad was demobilised in 1948, clothing was still rationed. His khaki green demob army blanket was tailored into a stylish suit for Mum, coupled with a cream frilly blouse made from the silky remains of a parachute. She felt and looked a million dollars.

## God's Provision

Auntie Irene, Mum's long-standing friend from schooldays, owned a fish and chip shop in Wellington Street, with her husband, Uncle Eric. Mum worked there, at times that allowed her to meet Tony and I from Gilmour Infants and Nursery schools, supplementing Dad's army pay as a lance corporal. Her job was peeling mountains of potatoes, in cold water, during freezing English winter weather. She would walk to Southbank Road School each afternoon, come rain or shine, pushing Stuart in the pram. On warmer days, she packed sandwiches and diluted National Health orange juice to picnic in Long Lane Park.

We even had holidays during those post-war summers. The local grocer, Mr Hill, owned a wooden bungalow in Tyn-y-Morfa, near Rhyl, North Wales. A small sum of money would be lodged with him each week between Christmas and summer to cover the bungalow rent. And food items were stored in a box at the bottom of Mum's wardrobe. Then, come the long summer holidays, we lugged suitcases laden with food and clothing to the local train station and headed for the seaside for two weeks. Dad was still in the army, but Nana came too.

The bungalow was a wonderful holiday spot for children, just sand dunes covered with blackberries between us and the sea! But it was more like camping in the bush for the adults— no electricity, so the house was lit by candles, no running water either. And I have no recollection of a proper stove for cooking. Those "holidays" would have been an endurance test for Mum and Nana. The toilet was a small freestanding cabin at the back of the cottage, and the "dead men" were buried before each family left. The child labour force did help collecting buckets of water from the communal taps, but we were oblivious to the real workload, running wild over the dunes and into the sea, building sandcastles on the beach, and picking blackberries.

Church services were held on Sunday mornings in the open field next to the convenience store. Occasionally, there was an open-air movie or singalong on Saturday nights. The family in the bungalow next door were regular visitors to Tyn-y-Morfa; they came from Manchester and owned a car! The Crosbys from Speke rented the bungalow opposite for several years at the same time as we did. Mum and Mary Crosby became friends. John and I were the same age. His birthday was on 16 July, a day after mine, so there were shared parties. I have no idea how Mum cooked, but there was always a birthday cake, and we came home to Liverpool tanned and healthy.

## Journey to Healing and Forgiveness

As the dust settled after the war, children in Liverpool and other bombed cities were identified as suffering from St Vitus's dance (chorea). Colomendy Holiday Camp in Wales had been a refuge for Liverpool's children since 1939—many evacuated there. In 1948, the camp was renamed Colomendy Convalescent Camp, and holidays were organised for both British and German children.

My brother Tony, born during Battle of Britain week, was diagnosed with St Vitus's dance. In 1950, he was one of those selected from Merseyside and Europe for convalescence. The children, who had all been affected by bombing, spent a fortnight in the Welsh countryside, enjoying outdoor activities under the supervision of athletics instructors and medical professionals. During those weeks, Tony made friends with some of the German boys. He brought Norbert home to our house in Earp Street after the camp for an extra few days' holiday. The two boys really bonded, despite language challenges, and they even looked alike with their blond hair and sun-bronzed skin!

The result of those two weeks in the Welsh countryside was little short of miraculous as the twitching, jerking, and fidgeting had stopped by the time Tony came home. Norbert's mother wrote a thank you letter to my mother, and another miracle happened. Forgiveness came as these two women, whose husbands served in opposing armies, struck up a friendship by mail that continued for years.

My mother was not a Bible-bashing Christian, but she did love God, and His love flowed through her to others. She worshipped in Church regularly and guided her children to live life God's way. Her faith cushioned me and my brothers from the horrors and after-effects of the Second World War.

# TWO

# A Time to Embrace

## Extended Family

Being the eldest in the family is a privilege but comes with expectations. During the years Dad was in the army, I was Mum's second in command! I learned to manage money from an early age, carefully counting change when sent with a list to do grocery shopping. One of my Nana's sayings still resonates: "Look after the pennies, and the pounds will look after themselves." Practical skills of sewing, cooking simple meals, and ironing using a flat iron heated on the stove were learned hands-on. I even learned how to wallpaper this way! When Mum spotted a single roll of wallpaper going at an absolute bargain price, we gave the living room in Earp Street a facelift. With just enough to cover one wall, the wallpaper was affixed, Mum at the top of the ladder, seven-year-old me at ground level. What a team!

Visits with Nana to her sister, my Auntie Lily, in Altrincham were highlights. I'd catch up with my married cousins, see new places, and take rides in Ken and Helen's sidecar. The downside was my travel sickness during the bus journey—so embarrassing! I was grateful Nana still took me along, and eventually I outgrew the problem.

Uncle Harold and Auntie Ada lived near Manchester with their gorgeous blonde twin boys, my cousins Alec and Howard. When I was nine, I travelled for part of the journey alone—Nana left the bus at Altrincham, and I was met by Auntie Ada three stops later. Independence! The plan was to spend the week of the November midterm holiday helping Auntie Ada with my toddler cousins. I'm not sure about the help I gave but it was a fun time with the twins. And I can still remember the excitement listening to the radio announcement of Prince Charles's birth on 14 November.

The Findlay clan were also close, and we had wonderful "cousins" holidays with Auntie Josie and Uncle Matt in Birkdale near Southport. Uncle Matt would drive his car to Liverpool collecting Pat and Ian from Aigburth and then Tony and me from Garston and drive us all back to Birkdale to join Cynthia and David at their place for a week of mayhem. The six of us ranged in age from eight to thirteen and blended well, mostly. Stuart, at four, was too young to join the tribe but contributed by mispronouncing our names, giving some nicknames that stuck. Cynthia was "Sinty" which she fine-tuned to Cindy. I was "Wowie"!

Each January, Auntie Josie would buy a pig, who was always named Curly Wee and kept in a pen in their garden, fed, and treated like a pet. Each year in December, Curly Wee would disappear. I can't recall ever questioning his disappearance or making any connection with the food on the table for Christmas! It was just what happened. Come January, there would be another Curly Wee.

## Scholarship

Towards the end of 1949, those carefree days of childhood took a downturn. I had reached the age when teachers started preparing pupils for senior school. There were three types of senior school, grammar, secondary modern, and technical. A scholarship exam, "eleven-plus", was the right of entry path to grammar schools. First, there was a review process, which determined which pupils, at the age of ten, could cope with the stress of a lengthy written exam. I was one of those selected, and our teachers groomed us for the eleven-plus exam held in February 1950.

Each student chose three grammar schools in order of preference, the actual exam to be written at the school of first choice. Aigburth Vale High School was my first choice, where friends Beryl and Audrey from my church were already pupils. My second choice was Calder High School, attended by other friends Joan and Muriel. Both of these schools were newish grammar schools built in the southern suburbs and within easy bussing distance for an 11-year old schoolgirl—no school busses were provided in England back in the day. My third choice was Belvedere High in the city, an upmarket private school that offered scholarships to a select few. Nannie and Granddad offered financial assistance if I didn't pass the exam!

On examination day, I travelled to school with Audrey and her sister Pauline who was also sitting the eleven-plus. Was I stressed? A little apprehensive of the unknown maybe, but I was not alone. There were about a hundred girls similar to me in age, plus a group of 14-year-olds from secondary modern schools who were retrying for grammar school places in Form 3. We were lined up in alphabetical order, chatting until herded into the examination hall.

Then there was a cliffhanging wait time before the final

results were announced in June. Those who were border line were called back in May—the dreaded recall! Several of my classmates were recalled, but not me. Did that mean Duncombe Road Secondary Modern would be my school for the next five years?

The results finally arrived, and my name was called! I had passed, gaining entry into the school of my first choice, AVHS. There were tears of disappointment for those who had failed and tears of joy for those who had been selected. We were dismissed from school early, and I raced home to tell my mother and, later, Dad.

During the long school holidays prior to starting high school, I developed psoriasis. No one associated the condition with the pressures of the high school selection process. My scalp was successfully treated by specialist physician Dr Bamba and cleared before school started in September. But over the years, psoriasis flared up again and again in times of stress and until I was healed, forty years later!

The long summer holiday of 1950 was bittersweet—the end of childhood. My two closest friends, Pauline and Betty, were not going to Aigburth Vale. Pauline had failed the entrance exam and would resit next year. Betty did not survive the review process and was headed for Duncombe Road Secondary Modern. Our days of walking to school together were over. Now we were at three different schools, a big chunk of our lives had changed. We still met up on Sunday at church and Wednesday nights for Girls' Life Brigade, but it was the end of an era.

## New Vistas, New Friends

First term started in September in summer uniform, which could have been straight from a fashion catalogue. We had a choice of sixteen dresses! There were four styles in four colours, light blue, green, yellow, and beige—all with the same trimmings around the neckline and shoulders but styles allowing for students' varying shapes and colourings. This was a far cry from some of the other dreary school uniforms. Three dresses were chosen in blue, green, and yellow. What luxury! Never could I remember having three brand-new dresses at one time. The winter garb was a navy blue serge V-necked tunic, made by Mum; a pullover; and gloves and scarf, all hand-knitted. Blazers were optional and expensive; my first one was a hand-me-down from Beryl, who also gave me her old tennis racquet. My birthday gift from the Findlay grandparents was a real leather satchel. I was good to go.

Some of the teachers are firmly planted in my memory! The principal, Miss Curry, was rather aloof and forbidding and called me "Marry" instead of "Maree." My history teacher was eccentric, volatile—nicknamed Totty Flip and given to standing on her desk and shouting. The sports mistresses were fun and a welcome relief during a six-hour day of study. Miss Skelley taught geography with a passion, planting dreams of faraway places in my mind.

The most memorable was, Sheila A, from Malta, newly qualified. She is someone I will always remember, for her sensitivity, her compassion, and the way she shared her faith as she taught scripture.

Students were drawn from all over Liverpool, and I made friends with girls from "posher" suburbs like Allerton and Hunts Cross. They gave me an insight into how other people lived, expanded my vision. Barbara P and I became friends over our shared love of tennis. Her family included me in excursions to watch motorbike racing, driving me home in their car. I was conscious of the difference between Barbara's lifestyle and mine when they delivered me back to our two-up, two-down rented home, before returning to their detached home with a garden. My future dreams began to take shape.

Did this wider vision also give me a snooty, better-than-you attitude? It was around this time I was allocated household chores designed to bring me down a peg. Cleaning the outside toilet was one of them and scrubbing our front door steps on Saturday mornings. Mum said she wanted the steps clean when people walked past for church. But years later, I recognised her wisdom. I would be on my knees scrubbing when friends and neighbours walked by—very humbling! But no chores /no pocket money, so I did my assigned jobs. And hopefully my attitude improved quicker than it would have as a result of Mum shouting at a know-it-all teenager.

## First Dance

Desks were tandem style, and mine was next to Margaret. She was quiet and shy and not sporty. We shared school lunches and compared church activities. Margaret invited me to my first dance when I was 14. Her church, All Souls, Springwood, was hosting a youth Valentine's Day dance.

This called for something new to wear, so Mum and I headed for Garston Market to buy material, and, with her help, I created and sewed my first dress. It was white with red polka dots, a pleated organza frill around the neck and shoulder line, a circular skirt, and a narrow red waspie belt. My brother Tony said I looked "a whole cheese". Mum surprised me with my very own lipstick, matching the dress colour! But all trace was scrubbed from my face before church the next day. Baptists did not wear make-up.

Edith, a friend from church was going to the Valentine's

Day dance, so we travelled by tram together, bubbling with excitement. There were strict codes of behaviour in the fifties. The girls all grouped together on one side of the hall, and the boys on the other, eying each other up. Girls did not ask the boys to dance—that would be considered "forward". Hearts beat faster each time a boy headed across the room—is he going to ask me to dance? The atmosphere could be tense! *Will he? Won't he? Oh no, not him. Yes! Yes! Ask me, not her!*

The Paul Jones dances were fun. Two circles walked in opposite directions; when the music stopped, you danced with the young man you were standing next to. Everyone dancing the Paul Jones had a chance to meet and dance with people they didn't know. The band was loud and lively, including young musicians who knew the latest hits.

By the time we reached refreshment break in the middle of the evening, tension was lessening, and conversations could be started. No alcohol on site, only cold drink and snacks.

It all ended at eleven with a last waltz, usually to the song "Last Waltz"! Occasionally, a girl tried to sneak off with one of the boys, but most just headed for the tram, as Edith and I did. A few were collected by parents or, like Margaret, walked home, with big sister Norah, tired but happy.

AVHS opened my eyes, enlarged my life vision, and introduced me to people from professions in higher incomes groups. New extramural experiences previously unknown were also revealed, among them tennis, gymnastics, theatre productions, and orchestral concerts.

My career goal during those school years was to train for something medical, nursing or radiography. I joined nursing cadets at Garston Hospital, mostly emptying bedpans but getting a glimpse of hospital life. Those grammar school years came to an abrupt end when my family moved to Rhodesia in 1955. The game plan changed, and I left school without sitting the GCE exam.

# THREE

## A Time to Tear Down

"They're here!" Excitement was tangible as we pushed and shoved down the passageway to the front door in time to see Uncle Harry easing himself from behind the wheel of the small hire car, followed by Uncle Vic, a friend from Rhodesia., (now Zimbabwe)

Stuart had been keeping watch all morning and now was holding back, suddenly a shy 8-year-old. His mum and his uncle were hugging—and crying—reunited from opposite ends of the earth.

Auntie Mattie, Arlene, and Graham somehow emerged from back of the car and were swamped by more hugs and shouts: "Look how big you are," to Graham, only 2 when they left England. "Your hair is so pretty and curly," to Arlene, a shy 5-year-old three years ago, now 8 years old and a still shy, despite her gorgeous auburn hair. "And so tanned!" True, Rhodesian sun and the two-week holiday on board ship had given them all a glow that this post-war English family did not have.

19

Everyone crowded into the tiny living room of our house at 14 Earp Street, talking non-stop, smiling, laughing, patting, hugging some more, and making up for three years of separation. A meal was laid out on the dining table, and we loaded our plates to talk as we ate.

The five cousins moved to the front room, used as a playroom. We tried to remember each other from three years ago. At 13, I had good memories of my younger cousins, who had lived with Gran Parker until she died four years ago. The timing coincided with Uncle Harry securing a post with an engineering company in Southern Rhodesia and moving his family there.

## New Vision

Mum and Dad hung onto every word as Uncle Harry described life in Rhodesia in glorious technicolour. "Uncle Vic" confirmed and embellished the stories; their intent was to encourage my parents to pack up and join them. And they succeeded.

Life in post-war Britain was hard for Betty and Les Findlay. Their rented house was dark and damp. But it was a roof over their heads, undamaged by bombing, so they did not qualify for one of the new state houses. These were allocated to those who had been bombed out and were living in rented rooms or with relatives. Now, my parents could see a golden future for the family, with sunshine all year round, help in the house, and a real garden instead of a backyard!

Uncle Harry helped Dad complete and submit his papers to apply for a work permit and residency, and the following year saw my father fly away to Africa. Long distance flights in 1954 landed at dusk each day, and passengers overnighted in

Malta, Entebbi, and Nairobi en route to Salisbury, Rhodesia. On the first leg of his journey, film star Jack Hawkins was travelling on the plane! Mattie and Harry's thatched pisé de terre cottage was bursting with two new immigrants. My cousin Tony Leigh had also been wooed away from post-war England and arrived a month before Les Findlay.

Dad's plan had been to work for a year, earning the money needed to buy passages for the rest of the family to travel by ship. But within seven months, he'd saved enough for the fares, and we were booked on the *Stirling Castle* for 17 February 1955.

Our family holidays had always been in self-catering cottages, so the prospect of two weeks on board a luxurious liner was both exciting and daunting! Clothes? Mum and I would need ball gowns for the captain's dinner dance—not something hanging in our wardrobes. The extended family rallied around. Auntie Josie made my first ball gown, pale blue tulle over taffeta with black velvet bows. Auntie Glad took Mum in hand, and they bought a lovely red strappy three-quarter-length dress, with a bolero—all the rage in the fifties.

Uncle Les and Auntie Glad did even more for us, taking Tony, Stuart, and me on a shopping trip to kit us out with summer weight pyjamas and other clothes more suited to a warm climate.

## Baptism

As the time grew closer to leaving, I wanted to be baptised at Garston Baptist Church. This had been our home church since the family had moved next door in 1941. Stuart had been dedicated there, and we'd each joined Sunday school as early as they would take us. Girls' Life Brigade for me and Boys' Brigade for Tony and Stuart were all part of our lives. The youth camps had been highlights. The prospect of leaving behind my church, and especially my friends, was heart-wrenching. I wanted them all there when I went into the waters of baptism.

Our pastor, Hugh J, agreed to guide me through the pre-baptism preparation, one-to-one, unlocking the meaning of familiar Bible verses. It was a valuable time and part of the grounding for my future life. I diligently took notes during our talks, started praying more intentionally, and began to keep a journal of "thoughts" about the readings.

One of my favourite hymns at that time was "I've Found a Friend", and we sang it often at Garston Baptist. I giggled, teenaged girl style, along with my friends at words about Jesus that could also be applied to boyfriend relationships. But the truth of those words resonated and impacted me:

> I've found a friend, Oh such a friend, He
> loved me ere I knew him
> He drew me with the ties of love, and thus
> He bound me to him,
> Still round my heart more closely tie the ties
> that ne'er can sever.
> For I am His and He is mine, forever and
> forever.

Pastor J included this hymn in the service and told the congregation that it was one of my favourites. The service itself is a blur in my memory; the night was typically English, extremely cold weather, and the water had been graciously warmed! Mrs Kilgallon, my Sunday school teacher for many years, helped me dress in white, and I felt nervous and excited. But did I really know the importance of this step I was taking?

My feelings since have been those of regret that there had been no Damascus road experience prior to baptism. Was I totally committed to Jesus in heart and mind? Or was this another step in my journey to a deeper relationship with the Lord? I know He has had His hand on me always. He *has* bound me with the ties of *His* love—even when I have been casual in my relationship. He is faithful and has held me close over the years.

My special friends were all at the service on that Sunday night. And my family, Mum, Tony, and Stuart; Nannie; and my godmother, Nana, were there, too. Nana gifted me my own complete Bible (King James version). It was leather bound and had tiny print, and she inscribed it, "With love from Auntie Nance." I still have it!

A real highlight was my Form 4 teacher, Sheila A travelling across town to be at my baptism. Her sincere faith had been evident as she taught scripture, bringing Luke's Gospel and Acts to life.

## The Big Move

By early January our home was dismantled as furniture was sold. Those household effects travelling with us were packed into tea chests and transported to the dock to go into the hold of the ship. We left the house in Earp Street that had been our home for fourteen years. Mum and the boys spent our last weeks in Auntie Nance's home in Woolton. I stayed with Nannie and Grandad in Speke, sleeping on their couch, Nannie fussing and spoiling me. As we left Earp Street and our church, Pastor Jenkins gave me an introductory letter to deliver to the pastor of Salisbury Baptist Church when we arrived—another link in the chain.

The night of 16 February was filled with painful goodbyes. Uncle Les drove Mum, Nana, Stuart, and the mountain of luggage to Lime Street Station. Tony and I caught the bus from Allerton Cenotaph to the city. As I tearfully waved goodbye to my friends Muriel, Joan, and Edith through the snow that had started falling, I realised this could be the last time I would see them—friends or snow!

When Tony and I arrived at Lime Street station, the overnight train to the port of Southampton was already at the platform, and our luggage was being loaded into the carriage. My mother's strength is coming to light on these pages! She was leaving behind her sisters, brothers, and lifelong friends, in reality breaking contact, as there was no internet in 1955 and few telephones where we were going. Letters took at least two weeks each way between England and Africa. What an epic upheaval for a five foot two woman—selling up her life's possessions and even some of her treasures and embarking on a 7,000-mile journey, over sea and land, with three self-centred children aged between 10 and 15!

*Betty Parker Findlay, you were one strong lady! It inspires me to know your strength came from your faith in the Lord.*

## Transition

The fourteen days at sea were a glimpse into a world not even imagined! It was a luxury holiday. Our family shared a four-bunk cabin. Tony and Stuart ate their meals in the children's dining room, but Mum and I were together in the main dining room, placed at a table with a honeymoon couple. There were two swimming pools, movies, dances, games, and fancy dress parties. It was the most amazing holiday ever—healing and restoring for my mother after the trauma of selling up and leaving family and friends. She made new friends with a Salvation Army family on board, the Lewises, whose four children were similar in ages to ours. We attended the ship's church services together and enjoyed the games and entertainment on board. Our first Rhodesian friends!

A young man in his early twenties, Stephen, travelling alone, attached himself to our family. He lived in Salisbury, and the letter of introduction from my pastor was addressed to his pastor at Salisbury Baptist Church! Was that a coincidence or a *God*incidence?

Shortly after the crossing of the line ceremony, there was an explosion in the engine room of the ship, causing alarm among the passengers. For two days, we drifted around the ocean while engineers worked in the heat to restore and repair the engine. Cheers broke out when the silence was broken by engines refiring, and we were, once again, heading for Cape Town.

The two extra days at sea were just an extension of the holiday to us children, but this caused rail connections to be rescheduled for the journey from Cape Town to Rhodesia. The train service was twice weekly, and late arrival meant we would miss the original booking. Mum handed our details over to the purser who undertook to sort out new train bookings and find accommodation for us in Cape Town. She was relieved to hear that this would be at Union Castle's expense!

## Arrival in Africa

It was midday when we disembarked in Cape Town, and the transport terminal was a hubbub of passengers, greeters, and piles of luggage. We three children were instructed to sit on a bench, guarding our luggage while Mum went to find a taxi. We waited as instructed, somewhat overwhelmed by the crowds, and were relieved when a man arrived, claiming to be a taxi driver sent to collect our luggage. He loaded some of the cases onto a trolley, saying he would be back for the rest, and we should wait there.

As he headed towards the entrance Mum returned, aghast when told that our luggage had been collected. She ran after the man, shouting, "Stop, thief!"

Tony ran in front of the trolley, stopping the thief, who ducked through the crowd and was gone.

The stalwart Betty Findlay was shaken—we all were, but she was the one navigating the whole operation! We went back to the bench to collect our thoughts and absorb the reality that we could have lost our last few possessions.

Eventually, we were all calm enough to be able to load another trolley and head out to the taxi ranks.

The purser had booked us into a charming little guest house at the foot of Table Mountain. The view of the town, the sea, and Signal Hill from our bedroom window was breathtaking. We took a stroll around the quaint houses before dinner—so different to the streets we knew in England. Then, early to bed, ready for the next step of the marathon journey.

This was to be three gruelling days by train, non-stop, through the changing countryside of South Africa, Botswana, and Rhodesia—small towns, desert, and larger cities. It would be three days cooped up in a carriage with no air-conditioning.

Money was running short by then, but a sleeper carriage had been booked and prepaid with four bunks, bedding, and two meals each per day. Mum bought some extras for lunches and snacks on the journey, and fruit was often on sale from vendors when the train stopped. We played I Spy, ad nauseum, and snakes and ladders and draughts with the Lewises. It was a long journey—an exhausting three days.

Excitement levels intensified as we neared Salisbury. As the train slowly eased into the station, the whistle blew long and loud—a celebratory blast

*We had arrived! Our new life was about to begin.*

# FOUR

## A Time to Rebuild

### New Home

Dad and Uncle Harry were waiting at the station to welcome us, with a car and a bakkie in the car park. The sky was clear blue, not a cloud to be seen! It was Stuart's tenth birthday, 9 March 1955, and our new life was about to begin.

After tea and catching up with Auntie Mattie, Dad took us all to view our accommodation. We could sense his anxiety. Cranborne Hostel had been RAF barracks during the war and was now used for housing and feeding immigrants, cheaply. Mum's optimistic facial expression did not waver as the door to our rooms opened. She looked around at the army type beds, bare wooden floors, and grey walls with high windows; smiled; and said, "We will soon have this looking like home!"

There were two adjoining rooms for five of us, no kitchen, and bathrooms were communal at the end of the block.

Mum certainly did her magic. Over the next days, tea chests were opened, and the furniture rearranged. Bedspreads and cushions were unpacked, turning the spartan beds into corner couches. A colourful rag rug made by Nannie Findlay hid a large chunk of bare floorboards, and pictures were hung on the walls. Pretty cloths covered the empty tea chests, making a kitchenette with kettle and tea things. It wasn't exactly home, but it was liveable until we were able to rent a house.

Auntie Mattie and Uncle Harry's home was in walking distance of the hostel, and initially the joint families decided I should share 11-year-old Arlene's bedroom, instead of crowding in with my brothers. This was hard for both of us, an intrusion on Arlene's space and I missed my family. So, the boy's bedroom was rearranged—wardrobes forming a dividing wall—and I moved into my corner.

## New Lifestyle

Tony and Stuart were registered at local schools, but I balked at returning to senior education. My parents were persuaded I should continue studying shorthand, typing, and bookkeeping in the evenings at Salisbury Polytechnic and look for daytime work to help the family budget. My career dream was still nursing, but in Rhodesia the enrolment age was eighteen with no cadet nursing in the interim—three years before training could start. I enrolled for a bookkeeping course at Salisbury Polytech. Auntie Mattie doubted I could find office work with very minimal office experience on my CV, but I felt confident and registered with an employment agency.

Imagine the delight when, within four weeks of arrival, I was employed as a junior typist in the mail order office of a large departmental store, the same store where my mother was working in the shoe department. A lovely Christian lady, Edith England, was in charge of the mail order department and took me under her wing, guiding me firmly but gently during those early days in a foreign land. Thirty years later, I met Edith again when we joined the same Bible study group.

## New Friends

Cranborne Hostel was the ideal restarting place for shy teens. Meals were eaten in the communal dining hall, where people could not be avoided, and we soon started making new friends. I bussed to work with Dorothy and Kathy, recent immigrants with their families. Dorothy and I worked at the same store and shared tea breaks. We both missed our churches "back home". So, one Sunday morning, we bussed into the city and attended service at Salisbury Baptist Church. Pastor Jenkins' letter of introduction was handed over, and we also met up with Stephen, the man from the boat. He introduced us to the youth pastor and set us up for youth group on Friday nights.

The downside of life at Cranborne Hostel was the food. It was really good, sustaining food and plenty of it! Cooked breakfast every day, sandwiches for lunch, and a hot meal at night. Wonderfully sustaining if you were a tradie, but added to the three weeks travelling and eating every wonderful thing that came my way, I began to pile on the pounds. How easy they are to pile on and how hard to take off again! Mum took control and monitored my food intake. In place of bacon and eggs for breakfast in the dining hall, we had fruit and cereal in our rooms, with a salad for lunch. This stopped the weight gain and started the slimming down process.

Cranborne Hostel offered fun opportunities for young people to enjoy their new life—dances or movies on Saturday nights. This was our home for six months until we moved into a modest house in Braeside. Life in Rhodesia was taking shape—a new home, new church and youth group, friends, work, and study.

## Headaches

Then, seemingly out of the blue, I suffered severe migraine headaches. This was not something I had ever experienced. The pain at night, and occasional vomiting, affected my sleep. I became anxious and then depressed. Mrs England noticed the change and suggested a visit to her doctor.

Dr Bernberg was a kind elderly Jewish man. He gently questioned me about leaving England and how I was adjusting to life in Rhodesia. He asked about work and how was I coping with the ongoing structural change and increased noise levels at work.

Noise levels? I had not associated the noise with migraines. The store owners were enlarging their premises, knocking down walls and removing windows, without closing their doors. The constant sound of hammering was added to the already invasive pneumatic tubular cash system. Dr Bernberg said the high noise levels could be the cause of those migraines. He suggested I look for another job, as the alterations were scheduled to continue for at least another year. Medication was prescribed for the migraines and also to deal with depression. However, he firmly told me there would be no repeats of the antidepressants.

The most valuable gift this dear doctor gave me was a piece of biblical wisdom to deal with depression—*as a man thinks in his heart, so is he*. He reminded me that I am in control of my mind and can turn those "poor-little-me" thoughts into expressions of thanksgiving. There is always something good to be thankful for even in the worst situations. I hung onto that promise, registered with an employment agency, and took the pills. For months, I kept the last pill in the bottle, before I accepted it was no longer needed and dropped it down the toilet.

## New Job

I resigned from the department store and started work with the Provincial Insurance Company. The company was privately owned by the Scotts, a Christians family from England's Lake District. The interview with the manager, Clive S, had included questions about my faith. The people I worked with all worshipped God in ways different to my Baptist way, but they did worship God; there were no atheists among the staff. One colleague, who became a good friend, was the daughter of a Pentecostal pastor; another was Jewish. Most were in church on Sundays. The branch manager, Clive, was a praying Catholic, as was the chief clerk, Charles.

There was an amusing incident when we were all invited to Charles's wedding. Clive and Dorothy's youngest daughter was so excited when Charles's bride arrived from England. At the reception, she asked, "Mummy, will I be a bride one day?"

Dorothy answered, "Oh yes. You will meet someone who loves you as much as Charles loves Pat."

Teresa was thoughtful. "What if I *don't*?" she asked at last.

"No problem," said Dorothy. "Then we will do what Ruth did!" Dorothy winked at me.

I had no idea what she was talking about and couldn't wait to get home and read the book of Ruth—discovering how she lay down next to Boaz and covered herself with his robe. I'm not sure if that was the right advice to give a starry-eyed ten-year-old girl, but it did get me reading my Bible again!

I loved my work at the Provincial and the people. My title was claims clerk/typist, and I was offered the opportunity to study for insurance diplomas. It wasn't just a job but the possibility of a career in insurance! The offices were light and airy. No noise, no more migraines—a promising new chapter.

# FIVE

# A Time to Search

## First Boyfriend

In addition to a new job, romance had come into my life.

While living at Cranborne Hostel, I met Ray, a quiet reserved young man. He asked me to a movie—my first ever date—and became my first boyfriend.

Ray was a "loner", not interacting with the larger group of young people at the hostel. Saturdays saw him revving up his motorbike and heading out of town towards Epworth or Domboshawa, sometimes with me riding pillion, clinging on for dear life! My mother, sensing he missed his own family back in South Africa often invited him to dinner with the family, and our dates were the movies on our own, not with the larger group. Occasionally, he could be talked into joining others for dance evenings.

One memorable night was the New Year's Eve dance at the State Lotteries Hall. This was a ticketed formal event; we made up a party with Kathy and others from the hostel group. And that was where I met Brian!

Ray was an excellent ballroom dancer—had attended

classes—but did not do the tango well. So, when the band struck up a tango, Ray opted to sit that one out. Brian walked across and asked me to dance. His girlfriend, Laureen, did not do the tango either. I was so impressed as this confident young man led me onto the floor. But I was soon disillusioned when he asked, "What is this one anyway?"

There we were, in the centre of an empty dance floor giving a demonstration of how *not* to dance the tango!

When Ray was called up for his National Service in July 1956, I wept buckets. And when the newspapers reported that Rhodesian forces could become involved in the Suez Crisis, I wept even more. Kathy and the group consoled me and included me in outings to movies or get-togethers in one of the homes. Brian was usually there, the centre of fun and laughter—his laugh was so loud, he couldn't be missed!

As the months went by and I realised I was enjoying fun times with friends and no longer missed Ray, I wrote a "Dear John" letter ending our relationship. My mother was furious. How could I be so cavalier with such a nice, gentle, kind young man as Ray, on his National Service? I knew this was not the kindest way to break up, but I also knew I was falling in love with Brian.

## New Boyfriend: Highs and Lows

The monthly dance at the Airways club was a highlight for our group of friends. Chris and Tony were engineers with the national airline and members of the social club. This gave us, as their friends, access to the monthly club dance, which became a regular on our calendars.

Another regular was picnic drives. The men all had sports cars; Chris and Isaac had MGs, Tony a Jaguar, Brian and Keith had four-seater Singer sports. On summer days, we would head off, hoods down, unphased by the dust roads, to swim at Zukanyika, boat at MacIlwaine, climb rocks at Epworth, or swim and slide on car tyres at Mermaids Pool.

Brian and I began "going steady". He attended church every Sunday and encouraged me to go with him to the Anglican Cathedral. These were very different services to those Baptist ones I was used to, but I enjoyed them. I appreciated the way the congregation was included in worship by the liturgy and was uplifted by the powerful organ and the choir singing. I also liked the controversial dean and attended his Wednesday lunchtime talks when he roasted local journalists. "The most common and destructive sin today is *idolatry*," he roared from the pulpit one Wednesday lunchtime. "Mr King, take note. I said *idolatry* not *adultery*." The shorthand outlines are the same!

Young reporter, Mr King sat behind a pillar taking notes—eager for something controversial to report in the *Herald*.

As our relationship deepened and became serious, Brian went through a time of uncertainty and soul-searching. Was he ready for marriage? He was not a tradie at heart but could see no other way to earn his living and felt trapped by the good income the building trade provided. His faith was deepening and growing, and he was attracted to, or intrigued by, the monastic life. These thoughts were incompatible with marriage; tensions increased between us, and we agreed to break up. I really loved Brian and thought this would just be a time apart to rethink our future, and we would get back together again in a week or two. But the weeks became months without contact.

During this time, I was asked out by several nice young men and encouraged by my mother to "cheer up" and accept their invitations. There were some pleasant evenings, but there was no spark. I was grieving over the break up and had pulled away from my friend group too. Kathy kept me in the loop and passed on any news she heard from Brian's friends. She told me that Brian had finally exited the building trade and was working for an insurance company in town. He was in training on three-month probation and mixing with a new crowd, including a girl called Cynthia!

I had stopped going to the cathedral to avoid contact with Brian, occasionally attending the little church in Cranborne—it was walking distance from home, and I knew no one there. Invitations from other suitors were a distraction. I focussed on my work and study. And after a few months, I believed I was getting over Brian and my life was on a more even keel.

Until, one lunchtime, rounding a corner into First Street, I bumped into Brian—literally. I was shaken by the depth of my feelings for him and dissolved into tears. Embarrassed, I allowed Brian to lead me into the Golden Arches for a coffee and talk. There was no suggestion we should make up, and I went back to work recognising this really was the end of our romance. I was heartbroken—a basket case really! I wept a lot and was generally unhappy. I stopped accepting any invitations—just stayed home.

## Healing the heartbreak

My parents decided a change of scene should help get Brian out of my mind. Mr and Mrs England were travelling down to South Africa on holiday, so Mum arranged for me to travel with them and have a holiday with my Southport cousins, now living in East London. The month spent with Uncle Matt, David, Cynthia, and her husband Norman gave me a new perspective and lifted my spirits, and I felt ready to resume life.

Uncle Matt had the bright idea of a boat trip for my return home—three days onboard ship followed by an overnight train journey from Beira to Salisbury. My poor mother was *not* in favour of this plan. Her 18-year-old daughter let loose on a cruise ship! But the plan was in place before she could stop it, and the prospect of a cruise liner was much more exciting than a car or plane ride.

The excitement started before we sailed. Uncle Matt had arranged for us to meet friends at a city restaurant for breakfast before heading to the docks. My ticket stated boarding time was 11 a.m., an hour before sailing time at midday. But a change to the port schedules brought the times forward an hour; sailing time would be 11 a.m., and boarding, 10 a.m. Passengers were notified by telephone—but we were not at home when the phone rang. With no cell phones back in the day, there was no way to communicate time changes. The shipping line were legally bound to contact *all* passengers before sailing, so they would not sail without me. We enjoyed a leisurely breakfast and shopped a little before heading to the docks.

Smoke was belching forth from the funnel and the horns were booming as we arrived at ten minutes to eleven! Two customs officials moved towards us and one asked, "Are you Marie Findlay?"

"That's me," I said, handing over my documents.

He barely glanced at them. "They are holding the ship for you. *Run!*"

Quick hugs all round, and the customs official grabbed my suitcase in one hand and my hand in his other and started running down the length of the dock. I was dressed in my best travelling outfit, fifties style, with high heels. Passengers were leaning over the ship's rails spurring me on!

"Keep going, girl."

"Take your shoes off."

I stopped, took off my high-heeled shoes, and ran in my stockinged feet. Cheers erupted as I reached the boarding platform—red-faced and panting. My documents and luggage were handed over, the gangway hauled in, and the ship began to move away immediately.

I found a place at the rails to wave to Uncle Matt and my cousins.

## Cruising the Indian Ocean

The ship's purser had placed this lone 18-year-old at a table with a group of lively young holidaymakers from Port Elizabeth, so every day was fun, fun, fun! I was the youngest, and all those handsome young men became very protective—especially when a crew member invited me out for a drink in Durban! He was a young table steward, originally from England, who had recognised my English accent among all the other South African ones.

That three-day journey stretched to eight days when the ship broke down in Durban on day two. Passengers were advised there would be an extra day in Durban for repairs to the ship. We were allowed to go ashore but instructed to listen for the ship's horn. This would summon us back when repairs where completed. But no horn sounded, and the extra day turned into an extra five days! Time to see the sights and even a show and form friendships.

The evening entertainment on board continued, and we enjoyed dances and quiz nights. Tall, dark, and handsome Barry Millar was very attentive! He looked so like film star Stewart Granger that one fellow passengers nicknamed him "Jimmy". Barry became my escort for onshore outings and held my hand during the movie *Boy Friend*. My broken heart was definitely healing.

Once the ship was repaired, we sailed to Lourenco Marques. A tour of the city during the day included the fascinating Continental Cemetery and the beautiful cathedral. Barry suggested we go into the cathedral and led me to a pew to kneel and pray together. That night, our table group went to a nightclub in Lourenco Marques, my first ever nightclub—loud live band, smoky atmosphere, small intimate dancing area. It wasn't a late night, as the transport back to the ship rounded us all up and took us "home" by midnight.

The following evening, we docked in Beira. The dinner dance was a special farewell for those disembarking in the morning, me included. Barry and the rest of the group would sail back home to PE—another four days of holiday for them, but mine was ending. We danced the night away. The top hit song was "Around the World"; we waltzed cheek to cheek, and Barry wrote on the final menu "Around the World in 8 days".

Another goodbye was looming.

## Return to Reality

The train to Salisbury did not leave until 8 p.m. in the evening, so there was a whole day to enjoy the sights of Beira. Barry took me to the station, and I settled into a carriage with other Windsor Castle passengers. We chatted and played rummy during the journey. A delay in Umtali,(now Mutare,) caused late arrival the following day, Sunday afternoon instead of Sunday morning. How would I get from the city to Braeside? But when the train pulled in, my parents were waiting on the platform. And so was Brian!

Lots to talk about and download when we arrived home.

Brian's job with the insurance company did not tick the boxes, so he left without completing his probation period. Just when my hopes were rising, he dropped the bombshell. He was heading down to St Stephen's Balla Balla the following day to look deeper into his calling to become a celibate priest! No mending of our broken romance. I wondered why he was here at all.

Mum and Dad wanted to hear all about the extended boat trip and were intrigued to hear about Barry. They pegged him as a holiday romance, until he arrived on our doorstep two weeks later. He was armed with letters, offering me employment in his brother's company and accommodation in his sister's home, with references from Barry's church minister. He asked me to make the move to Port Elizabeth and pursue our relationship further.

My dad was distressed at the prospect of his only daughter leaving home, settling in South Africa, and possibly marrying this man who they had only just met. Barry stayed with the family for a week, a romantic week. He went home with my promise to think it over.

My final bookkeeping exam was looming, so it was time to get my head down and study. I had no idea what I was going to do next. As promised, I gave a lot of thought to moving to Port Elizabeth. Was I ready to take such a step of commitment?

Then Brian came back.

# SIX

# A Time to Keep

## Return

The six weeks spent at the monastery had given Brian a time to think and pray and had cleared a lot of misconceptions. The monks had counselled and guided him so that he was closer to seeing the life God had intended for him. Monastic celibate life was definitely not his calling! (I could have told him that!) The time spent at the college attached to the monastery studying in their libraries had opened his eyes to the possibility of teaching. How that could happen, he had no idea. So, he prayed about it, wrote it in his journal, and left it on the back burner. He also discovered how much he missed me and wanted to rekindle our relationship.

Until the trip to Balla Balla, Brian had been living with his parents. But their home was crowded, and their lifestyles were different, prompting him to look for digs. He was both concerned and irritated that his mum had given up her job with a department store and was "always sleeping". Eventually, the reason was revealed. Vera Bishop was pregnant and not coping physically or emotionally. When Michael Trevor was born in January 1958, the new addition brought great joy to his parents' lives.

Church House in the Avenues provided accommodation for single young men and cathedral priests and had a room available. John White, a young priest aged 27, became a friend and mentor. A private hotel across the road provided meals for the residents. Brian went back on the tools, doing what he knew best but chose to work with a smaller jobbing service, choosing maintenance over construction. He was able to extend his work hours and earn a good salary—enough to plan for the future.

## Engagement

Shortly after Christmas, we both realised we were in love and wanted to spend our lives together. In February, Brian "popped the question", and on Saturday 28 February, our friends were all invited to my home for buffet dinner before heading for the monthly Airways dance. Auntie Matty, Uncle Harry, cousin Tony, Vic, and Muriel were sharing dinner at Mum's, so our engagement was announced to the assembled family and friends—champagne corks popped, my sapphire and diamond ring displayed. It was a lovely celebration, followed by our favourite dance night.

The wedding of my Jewish friend, Ruth to Raffy was the following day, 1 March, and she was delighted to read our engagement announcement in the paper on the morning of her wedding. Our engagement was also celebrated at the preparation for communion service on the following Saturday evening; the dean blessing the ring and our commitment to each other. No date was set for the wedding at the time of our engagement; we anticipated more than a year to prepare ourselves.

## The Wedding

The preparation period changed when Dad accepted a promotional transfer to Sinoia. My mother was not comfortable with her daughter going into digs, so our wedding date was brought forward to 6 December 6, a month before they left Salisbury. That made for a nine-month engagement—enough time to make wedding plans and save for a honeymoon.

Kathy and Diana agreed to be my bridesmaids, together with my cousin Arlene and Brian's sister, Rosemary; Brenda at 10 was to be the flower girl. Brian's best buddy Tony would be his best man.

The cathedral was where we wanted to make our vows, with Holy Communion, which meant I would need to be confirmed. Confirmation classes started in June and provided a season of Bible study and restructured prayer time. I recommitted my life to God and confirmed my baptismal vows on 28 October.

Dates were also set for pre-marriage talks with the dean, who recommended books for us to read and gave valuable advice—some of which I remember still:

- "Never say never and never say always!" (For example, "You are always late for dinner," or, "You never put your clothes in the laundry basket.")
- "Do not let the sun go down on your anger" (Ephesians 4:26, NASV)

The final talk was an evening shared with the other four couples who were being married in the Cathedral on the same day; we discussed punctuality and flower arrangements. Again, the dean shared valuable information—that current statistics in Rhodesia showed that three of the five couples would divorce! He led us in closing prayer. We each prayed *not* to be one of the three.

## Planning for the Day

There was a wedding boutique in the arcade below the Provincial offices, and many lunchtimes were spent browsing. Wedding gowns were priced astronomically high, out of my budget. I was considering making my own dress, when Ruth told me of a family friend who wanted to sell her gown. The idea of a second-hand wedding dress did not appeal, but Ruth insisted the dress would be perfect for me, so I agreed to look. We drove to the friend's house after work one evening. And Ruth was right. The dress was everything I wanted for my wedding—beaded lace, a voluminous skirt, and it fitted perfectly as though made for me. And all for a price I could afford!

Peacock blue was agreed as the colour for the bridesmaids' dresses—it suited all their colourings, and they trusted me to make them! Flower girl Brenda would wear white. Mum chose dusty pink guipure lace for her mother of the bride dress, the colour she wore for her own pre-war wedding.

Catering would be by our friends Stan and Val and their new catering company. A hall was hired large enough for the 120 guests. Dad's band was the obvious choice for the reception music, and he also sourced the wedding cars, supervising my brothers attaching ribbons on the day. It was a family affair.

On the day, we left home at 10.30 a.m. to arrive at the cathedral on time. The white beribboned car attracted hoots and waves from passers-by as Dad and I were driven through Saturday morning shoppers. I returned with a royal wave, like the queen. The service of nuptial mass started at 11 a.m., officiated by the dean and assisted by our friends, John W and

Noel. It was a combination of pomp and traditional ceremony that we had wanted for our special day.

This was followed by a lunch, speeches, and dancing—and a dramatic moment when the three-tiered cake started to topple during the cutting ceremony! It was rescued by those standing by but in the foray, and my pearls broke and scattered across the floor. These were pearls brought home by my father from Japan and had been kept for me to wear on my special day. The pearls were gathered from the floor but when restrung, the necklace was shorter; some had been missed and left on the floor for the cleaners to find!

I changed into my going away outfit around four, complete with the hat and gloves of the day. We drove away, cans trailing the car and a "Just Married" sign on the back, heading for Enkeldoorn! Not the usual choice of wedding night venue but an hour's drive from Salisbury, the first of three stopovers on the 1,200-mile journey to Durban.

On the morning of day three, I could not hide my tears as we headed for the car. Brian thought I was finding the long journey too much, but I was just overwhelmed with happiness, sharing every moment with my new husband and the realisation that, one day, it would all end! We had said "until death us do part"; so, one day all this happiness would end.

## Honeymoon

Ten days had been booked in a sea front hotel, the Majestic. The brochures showed an upmarket vibrant hotel, with smiling well-dressed couples enjoying the facilities. But it was very different to the hotel we entered on 10 December! The lounge was full of old people sitting and reading and nodding off; wheelchairs were parked in the corridors! It definitely wasn't the atmosphere we'd been anticipating. I felt as though I needed to be on my best behaviour amid the sombre furnishings and hushed tones in the dining room with soothing background music.

Hope, Charlie, and Tommy, Tony Bayford's family, had missed our wedding due to their Christmas holiday plans made, before we brought our wedding date forward. They were staying at the Coogee Beach Hotel around the corner from the Majestic, one road back from the seafront. We joined them for lunch, delivering some wedding cake and telling them all about the day they had missed. We also shared our sad story of the geriatric Majestic Hotel, contrasting with the happy family sounds in the lively Coogee Beach dining room.

Hope was sad for us and told the manager our plight. Coincidentally, there had been a cancellation that very morning. A double room was available—no sea view, but the Manager offered to change the two single beds for a double for honeymooners. Our sort of place! The booking deposit we had paid to the Majestic covered the nights we'd stayed there, so we went back, packed our bags, and moved to the lively Coogee Beach family hotel. We spent our first married Christmas at the Coogee Beach, enjoying dances and movie nights at no extra cost! The difference in tariff meant we were able to extend our honeymoon by another week.

The long trek back home to Rhodesia started on 27 December, again a three-day journey, with stopovers in Petersburg and Bubye River—eaten alive by mosquitoes! We arrived home on 30 December, in time for the New Year's Eve celebrations.

Then we settled into our Rose cottage, unpacking wedding gifts, writing thank you letters, and looking at the wedding photos. Back to work on 5 January. Mum and Dad moved to Sinoia later in the week, and we settled into married life, still in honeymoon mode.

## Change Coming

On the evening of 26 February 1959, as we ate our dinner at our new dining table, we heard *beep, beep, beep; beeeep, beeeep, beeeep; beep, beep, beep*—SOS—the Rhodesian alarm signal on the wireless!

Our hearts sank as we listened to instructions for Brian's reserve regiment—summoned to report to the KG V1 Barracks the following morning. No details were given other than a state of emergency in the federation.

When I arrived at work red-eyed and still sniffling after saying goodbye to Brian, my new colleague Veronica was in the same state. She and her husband, Roy, had married the same day Brian and I had. When she started her new job at the Provincial in January, we had not known that our husbands had been in the same National Service intake. Now they were both on call-up in the same battalion. Veronica was living in Hatfield with her in-laws, so we travelled together to and from work during the time we were "grass widows".

There was no contact with the men as they travelled around Nyasaland. At last a phone call hinted that the end of duty was approaching, no specific date. Not many days later, we heard the distinct sound of Dakotas flying over the city. Were they carrying troops? The phone calls eventually came, and Veronica and I left work early, heading to the barracks to welcome our husbands home.

They were tired, dirty, and disillusioned, having seen very little action, more a show of force and peacekeeping. *But* we had all been given a glimpse of the uncertain changing times we were living through and a warning of difficult days ahead.

Betty Parker, soon to be Findlay

Les Findlay

Muriel, Eileen, Marie, Joan and Shiela –
Garston Baptist Friends

Family holiday at Tyn-y-morfa, Marie, Betty, Stuart and Tony

# SUMMER

# SEVEN

# A Time to Dream

## Life in Colonial Africa, as I Knew It

I interrupt the trips down memory lane to share some background for the next season, especially for those who have never experienced life in Africa.

My second grandson, a history scholar, sees many of my generation as Eurocentric colonialists. And there may be truth in his assessment. I was a colonialist inasmuch as I was a privileged white-skinned person living in a country populated mostly by black-skinned, underprivileged people—although truly, we are all shades of brown!

In 1955, when my family moved from England to Rhodesia, the people groups were labelled blacks (African), whites (European), and coloureds (mixed races and Asians). There were designated suburbs and services in the urban areas for each people group. As immigrants, my family accepted the status quo; this was the way things were done in Rhodesia. This was our first experience of living among people of other races; the only other nationalities I had met in Liverpool were Scottish, Welsh, and Irish!

As a Rhodesian émigré, I met few black people, and those I met were household servants. Even postmen and bus drivers were white back then. State schools and colleges were segregated, so childhood friends would be of the same shade. There was also the language barrier. English was the official language. Education from senior school level was in English, while junior students were taught in the vernacular of the main tribes. Afrikaans and Portuguese were spoken by sectors of the white population. From this mix evolved Chilapalapa, a mutated language that facilitated communication between people of all the tribes and races, similar in usage to pidgin in Malaysia.

This all sounds primordial by today's standard But in 1955, Rhodesia was still evolving. My grandson is probably right. As an immigrant from Britain, I had entered the country under the protection of the very people who had taken the land from the three feuding tribes in 1890. Sixty-five years had passed since the Pioneer Column had arrived with a handful of raw white settlers.

Rhodesia in 1955, although still a young under-developed country by Western standards, provided schools and hospitals for all its peoples. Main roads were tarred, and a railway network served all major cities. There was a national airline, a power grid in towns, and a massive hydro-electric project under construction at Kariba—impressive development in sixty-five years.

The indigenous peoples had their tribal lands outside of the cities, with acreage under their chiefs, to grow food and to retire to. *But* they had been jettisoned into the twentieth century, and their horizons widened—like it or not!

## Brian's Big Dream

In 1959, horizons widened for Brian and me too when we moved from the city of Salisbury to Domboshawa, in the Chinamora Tribal Trust Lands.

This all started with Brian's big dream. He was not a head-in-the-clouds day-dreamer, but he did have dreams. He was a man who believed that God could and would follow through when He put an idea into your mind! And God had given him a dream. His first career as a carpenter and joiner was his father's vision, never Brian's. He mastered the skills, worked hard, and completed a five-year apprenticeship while studying at Polytech for a building diploma. Carpentry provided a good living but was not his passion.

Essentially an academic and a deep thinker, Brian wanted his life to be spent in some meaningful way, doing God's will but was not sure what that looked like in terms of earning his daily bread. Six weeks were spent in prayer and seeking God's guidance at St Stephen's Monastery, Balla Balla. When he returned to Salisbury, he was holding onto a vision God had given him of the place he would work in the future. He accepted that he would not be a monk or a priest. Neither would he be working on the tools for his entire life. But possibly, he would be a teacher, living in the country. God had given him a vivid dream of the place he would live.

## Glimpse of a New Future

After our wedding in 1958, we settled into a strange little rented "cottage", part of a larger house. This was really just a room surrounded by a converted veranda with a bathroom shared with two other tenants. We chose this oddity in preference to an apartment with all mod cons because it was out of town and on three acres of rose gardens! Using his carpentry skills, Brian softened the spartan look, with flower boxes at the front door and a screen wall inside the entrance sectioning off the kitchen area. We loved our first home. But his big dream had taken root, and he was looking for change.

In October 1959, a small ad in the newspaper announced an opening for an instructor in carpentry at Domboshawa Training Institute. Brian eagerly wrote a letter of application, and we waited on tenterhooks for a response. He was called for an interview, during which a visit to Domboshawa was recommended, for both applicant and family. Living in the bush so far from town's amenities would require commitment.

We planned a day trip for the following Saturday. This was, for us, unchartered territory. We drove along the old Borrowdale Road, passing through farmland, and headed towards the Chinamora Tribal Trust land, twenty-five miles from the city. As we travelled, the road shrank, from full tar to nine-foot tar to strips and then to dirt.

The college had opened in 1940, sited in a rocky tribal area, intended to attract the local indigenous population for training in farming practices, health and hygiene, and building. The soil was poor sandy loam. But as it was cultivated, the land on the college side of the Domboshawa Road became lush and green, in stark contrast to the sandy desert on the village side, yielding spindly mealies.

We turned into the college through the impressive stone gate posts. Two mounted horsemen pulled to one side and raised their hats as we passed. I waved back regally, loving the place already. The dirt road swung in a gentle arc through grasslands, easing into what we later learned was referred to as the Royal Mile! It was a straight road, dirt but well graded, leading to a parade ground with a flagpole flying the

Union Jack (still British in 1959). The principal's house, with verandas on all sides, was immediately behind the parade ground, nestled into a lovely garden. Brian's face was a picture of excitement and expectation. He recognised the Royal Mile as the place in his dream! No question—if they would have us, we were coming.

The acceptance papers came two weeks later, and we packed with eager anticipation of starting an entirely new life. Our childhoods in different parts of post-war suburban Britain had been similar—crowded terraced houses without gardens. The move to Rhodesia had expanded visions for both the Bishops and the Findlays, but actually living outside of the city, in the country, had never been on our agenda. Until Brian's dream! We packed and prepared for the big move, anticipating a change in the way we lived but not knowing how big that change would be.

## Domboshawa

All our worldly goods were transported by the college truck, and we were allocated a small staff house, half a building that had formerly been a clinic. The living rooms, kitchen, and bathroom were accessed from the veranda. Two bedrooms led off the living room. The lighting on the veranda was minimal, just one bulb each end. The alcove beside the kitchen gave me my first introduction to bats! They hung from the ceiling outside the kitchen door, waiting to take to the air, swooping around heads.

Students were all indigenous males; entry was by scholarship examination, and successful scholars were fully funded by the government, including all living costs, uniforms, and sports equipment. Most of the students came from rural village families. And at each intake, Brian would raid his own cupboard for shoes and underwear not provided.

The college routine was based on colonial/military lines. The day started early with outdoor exercises. Then reveille assembled the college for the raising of the flags. The school anthem was sung as the flags were raised—"Dombo Dombo Domboshawa". Flags were lowered again each evening to the "Last Post" played on a bugle by one of the students. Very colonial!

Another colonial event was "afternoon tea". Lessons ended at 4 p.m., and staff went home for afternoon tea. As newbies, we were invited to each home in turn to welcome us or maybe to show us the ropes—best china and home-baked cakes! After tea, it was expected that the men, and some wives, would play a round of golf before dinner. Brian bought a second-hand set of clubs and a rule book and embraced the challenge. I became his caddy and walked the course, set in beautiful surroundings bordered with forest and mountains.

## Barrenness

This was also a time of heartbreaking disappointment, when we discovered babies were not going to come easily for us. Numerous examinations, procedures, and tests gave us little hope of a baby. IVF was newly available, as AIH or AID, but we had reservations. So, we approached social welfare to investigate adoption.

There were interviews, questionnaires, and references, and a lovely lady was appointed as "our" officer. Our names were added to the waiting list, estimated to be up to five years long! Prospects of becoming parents any day soon looked bleak, but I clung to the hope that, surely, there would be a miracle pregnancy along the way, long before the waiting time ended.

We had cut back on attending Sunday church services at the cathedral in town; twenty-five miles on dirt roads in our old Morris Minor was quite a trek! Twice a month, the priest in charge of Borrowdale parish would celebrate Holy Communion at the little chapel on the college campus. Brian and I attended these services and the combined services for students and staff in the hall, but we missed the sense of "belonging" to the cathedral and missed our friends.

## Faith Upheaval

Brian's faith had been severely shaken by his test results related to our childlessness. He felt cheated and angry, declaring this was not what God intended for him. He began questioning and embarked on a journey to discover God's healing power. One of his colleagues, Richard H., was a Christian Scientist and encouraged Brian to attend Sunday meetings with him.

The Christian Science approach is that all sickness is an illusion and can be resolved by prayer alone and right thinking. Richard gifted a copy of Mary Baker Eddy's *Science and Health: With Key to the Scriptures*. Brian stopped going to Anglican Church Services when he read the Christian Science take on Holy Communion. Mary Baker Eddy had written, "Our Eucharist is spiritual communion with the one God. Our bread, 'which cometh down from heaven,' is Truth. Our cup is the cross. Our wine the inspiration of Love, the draught our Master drank and commended to his followers." And Mrs Baker Eddy also provided the spiritual meaning of Holy Ghost—not the third person of the Trinity but "Divine Science; the development of eternal Life, Truth, and Love."

Now I felt angry too, and hurt, as though my whole world was crumbling! The kingpin of our relationship had been our shared belief in God. From our earliest dating days, I believed that Brian and I were on the same page. God had given me a husband who shared a faith like my own. I had envisaged our life unfolding, attending church together and raising a godly family; I would never be sitting on my own in church as my own mother had done! But now, we could not even pray together without a row starting. Brian was walking away from "our" church.

No way would I attend the Christian Science meetings.

"If you're not going to church, neither am I!" was my puerile, self-centred response.

I could have sat next to my husband in the Christian Science church, praying for God's wisdom and giving him support and understanding as he sought answers, but instead, I stubbornly stayed at home, seething.

My reaction to Brian's search for healing put a grave strain on our marriage, almost ended it. My face was turned away from the Lord, starting a spiritual decline.

And it thrust me into the wilderness years.

# EIGHT

# A Time to Laugh

## Hope in the Wilderness

Amid this time of turbulence in our marriage and faith journeys, there came rays of sunshine. One evening, the radio programme playing in the background was interrupted by the alert signal—*Beep, beep beep, beep, beep, beep; beep, beep, beep;* (SOS).

This is the signal used by the RBC to gain everyone's attention. And it did! We were eating dinner at the time and stopped, waiting anxiously to hear a vital message to the nation. Relief flooded us that it was not a national disaster and, thankfully, not another call-up or a weather warning. It was a cry for help by the Rhodesia Children's Home. Their building was in dire need of repair and reroofing; the SOS was to find suitable placements for all 100 children before the long Christmas school holidays started in three weeks.

Fostering had not been offered by social welfare, not even mentioned, so this was something new to us. Brian and I were longing to be parents, and I envied our friends with children, married in the same year as us. Our names were on the adoption list. But there could be a five-year wait before we had children in our lives. We listened with interest and discussed the possibilities.

"We have a spare bed," said Brian. "We could take a child. Could be fun for him on the farm."

Our home at the Training Institute was on a 6,000-acre farm. The staff houses were village style amid fields of maize and paddocks for jersey herds and sheep. Milking sheds, chicken runs, and pigpens were a short walk away at the farm. There were stables for horses and outcrops of rocks to climb. This could be a boy's paradise! Our neighbours had a son, and we began to picture another young boy fitting into the picture perfectly.

I telephoned the children's home and was told they desperately needed someone to take two little girls, sisters of 4 and 6.

"We only have one spare bed," I said.

"They are not very big," replied the matron. "They can sleep top and tail."

A trial weekend was arranged.

## Parenting/Fostering

The following Friday afternoon found us waiting in the matron's office for a practice run with the girls, before committing to the seven-week Christmas holiday. The door opened slowly, and shy 6-year-old Fay slipped in. She was dressed in a brown-and-yellow checked dress, which complimented her gorgeous strawberry blonde hair. Her head was down, wary of these strange people, nervous and clutching the familiar hand of her house mother. Attempts at conversation were stilted. There was no eye contact, no response to our greetings, just nods of the head. This could be a very quiet weekend.

Then 4-year-old Gail arrived! Her giggles could be heard down the corridor as she raced "Auntie Bessie" to the office and burst through the door—red hair flying, red cheeks glowing. We were introduced as Auntie and Uncle and headed out to the car. Fay was visibly anxious, but it was all an adventure to Gail. She waved happily to Auntie Bessie, blowing kisses as we drove away.

That weekend in November was a first for all of us. Gail had been 18 months old and Fay 3 when they were first moved into the Children's Home, almost three years earlier. Now, at 4 and 6, this was the first time they had been to stay with strangers, away from familiar surroundings. And it was our firsttime parenting. In hindsight, I am grateful they had each other, as I don't believe we shaped up well as stand-in parents!

The days were filled with fun and games and visits to the farm to see the animals and collect milk and eggs. Sunday came round quickly, and as we headed back to the children's home, there were sniffles from Fay in the back seat—a good sign after her wary, anxious start! The smiles peeped through as we hugged and said goodbye, promising we would be there in two weeks for the start of the long school holiday.

So, we had two weeks to get the room ready. Another bed was found and pretty covers made from striped sheets. The Dolly Varden dressing table that had been mine as a teenager was re-frilled and drawers lined with pretty paper. I was completing a short-term contract, working with my old company in the city, so lunchtimes became scavenger hunts for Christmas gifts and materials to make play clothes. The play clothes at the children's home were pooled, not specific to each child. I wanted Fay and Gail to have their own. The excitement of a Christmas with two children hanging up their stockings really kicked in! We had planned to spend the five days over Christmas in Chinhoyi with my Mum and Dad, and they happily took on the roles of foster Granny and Grandpa, with gifts under the tree.

That Christmas holiday was the start of regular weekend and school holiday foster care. Brian and I grew to love those little girls so much we felt the wrench each time they returned to the Rhodesia Children's Home. Could we make this permanent? An appointment was made with Mrs S at social welfare to discuss adoption. But this was not permissible under Rhodesian law, which stated adopted parents needed to be twenty-five years older than the children. I was too young! Permanent foster care was suggested as an option, and forms were completed there and then. The matron was told of our application, and we waited eagerly for the response. This was not what we had expected. Our next weekend visit was cancelled, and we were told the girls were leaving the Rhodesia Children's Home immediately to live with their mother.

Our request to adopt the girls had prompted their mother, Chris, to speed up her plan for them to live with her. Places were found at Avondale Primary School, walking distance from her flat, and the future for Fay and Gail looked bright. Bleak for us! There was no contact, no feedback on how they were enjoying their new life. Did they miss us as much as we missed them? There was no way of knowing. We could only thank God for the years we had shared them and pray for their happiness and fulfilment. Brian and I knew their mother's care was the best thing for Fay and Gail, but our lives felt empty—there was a huge void where "our" girls had been.

## More Parenting/Fostering

Shortly after this wrench, another child came unexpectedly into our lives at Domboshawa. We had moved into a new staff house and put the word out that we needed help to tame the surrounding bush into a garden. A rather small, 12-year-old boy named Aggrey applied. He told us his sad story. His mother had been diagnosed with tuberculosis and was now in the hospital at Makumbi Mission. He had nowhere to stay, as his relatives in Chinamora could not accommodate another child. He was looking for gardening work, with a place to stay, until his mother was well. I had been hoping to employ a big strong man to help with the garden not a young boy who needed care. But the staff accommodation attached to our house was empty, and we agreed to take him on.

Aggrey's schooling, or lack thereof, was a source of concern. Our friends, Peta and James had started a junior school for local children on their property in Glen Forest and offered a place for what would be Aggrey's last year at junior school. They found him to be a bright boy and eager to learn. So started a new season in life for Aggrey and for us. An old bicycle was borrowed on a "long lend" basis, and he rode to Glen Forest School each day, about three kilometres each way. Homework and some gardening in the afternoons; Saturdays were the main gardening days. We supplied his meals and gave him pocket money for his help in the garden. On Sundays, he took the bus to Chinamora and visited his mother in hospital—sometimes cycling the ten kilometres to keep the bus money!

One Sunday, he didn't return. No Aggrey, no bike! His clothes were still in his room, so he intended to come back. Had there been an accident? There was no way of directly contacting his relatives at Chinamora, no phone service from our house. Messages were sent through other staff on Monday evening, but no news came. Just when we were planning to visit the police station, he appeared at the door with the heartbreaking news that his mother had died.

We marvelled that he was so controlled for a young lad. No sign of tears or falling apart. He rode off to school each morning and tackled the gardening and homework in the afternoon, putting on a very brave face. Was it Shona custom to hide one's feelings so completely? Those regular Sunday trips to Chinamora were no longer needed, but he visited family there occasionally. As the year progressed, we asked, What next?

Peta offered to investigate options for senior schooling when Aggrey finished his standard 5 year with Glen Forest. For many Shona youngsters without education, work life started at 13—not what we wanted for Aggrey. He would need to write public exams and be assessed for a place at a secondary school.

Then one Saturday morning, we heard shouting in the garden. An angry lady was smacking Aggrey around his head as he stood in the veggie patch. What had he done? Brian called out, "Amai! Amai!"

She came towards us and held out both of her hands in greeting.

"This boy of mine never comes to see me anymore," she said.

"Your boy?" asked Brian. "Is Aggrey your son?"

"Yes. And he should be coming home with me, now."

The story unfolded. Aggrey knew he was in trouble for staying away extra days over the weekend and needed a really good excuse. The death of his mother was the only excuse he could think of that would work. And it did! But that also meant he could not borrow the bike or take the bus on Sundays to visit his mother, if she was no longer alive. A series of lies had ensued.

Amai was very angry when she heard he had reported her death. She had, in fact, been cured and released from hospital and was planning to return with her son to their own village.

Her husband had died some years earlier, so Aggrey was her sole responsibility and future support. She told Brian that, if her husband had been alive, he would have given Aggrey a beating for telling such a lie and asked Brian to give him the hiding he deserved.

Brian took Aggrey to another part of the garden, talked to him for a while, and then put him over his knee and gave him six of the best—school master style.

Aggrey cried then, sobbed and apologised to us and his mother. They packed up his belongings and headed away, ending a challenging but enriching year. We lost touch entirely—never heard from Aggrey again.

Until forty years later, that is.

*Tring, tring, tring; triiiing, triiiing, triiiing*—the party line phone rang in our Greystone home. The year was 2003. We were in the throes of packing to emigrate to New Zealand.

"Is this Mrs Bishop? Mrs Brian Bishop?" a man's voice asked.

"Yes it is," I replied, expecting a call from the travel agent.

"You may not remember me. I am Aggrey, Aggrey Mhlanga!"

Silence on the line as I moved out of emigration mode onto memory lane. "Aggrey! How wonderful to hear your voice. How did you find us?"

"The phone book. I called all the Bishops in the phone book!"

I could hear him taking a deep breath - was he going to ask for money?

"That time with you at Domboshawa keeps coming into my mind," he said. "Did I ever thank you for looking after me?"

We talked for a long time. I was thrilled to hear that he held an executive position with one of the large companies—he was a successful businessman. And in our conversation I also heard his faith in Jesus coming through.

That telephone call was a blessing and encouragement to me. There had always been questions. Had I done enough? Food and schooling yes, but had I shown love for that young boy? Was Aggrey part of God's plan to give me the opportunity to be a parent without actually producing a baby? Had my Heavenly Father been testing me to check if I could show enough love and care for children not carried in my womb?

Aggrey had come into our lives as Fay and Gail left to be with their mother, helping to fill the gap. When he left, we were once again a childless couple.

## "Chance" Encounter

One Wednesday, our Domboshawa shopping-in-town day, I was standing at the pay desk of a department store when there was a tug on my skirt. I looked down into Gail's bright blue eyes! We hugged and hugged; some tears from me. The lady with Gail looked on bemused.

"Your daughters stayed with us when they were in the Rhodesia Children's Home," I explained, pulling myself together as Gail leaned into me.

"Gail is not my daughter," the lady said "She is staying with me for the half-term holiday. She lives at Emerald Hill Children's Home."

We hugged again, and I whispered to Gail that we would see her again, very soon. What an amazing coincidence was that meeting with Gail. Or was it a Godincidence?

An appointment was made with the Mother Superior at Emerald Hill Children's Home. "What happened?" we asked. We heard how their mother, Chris desperately wanted her daughters with her. But her salary was low, and she soon realised she could not care for her daughters as she had hoped. And there was no one to care for them during the school holiday. Her friend Agnes encouraged her to investigate Emerald Hill Children's Home, which was not far from her flat. The girls had been christened Catholics, and Christine's application was accepted.

It was another upheaval for two little girls who had already been through so much. Mummy packed their bags, promised to visit them every weekend, and took them to Emerald Hill Children's Home, a totally new environment. Their carers were nuns, dressed in black, and the routine, typical of convent life, centred around prayer and discipline. This was a very different lifestyle to anything these young girls had ever known, but the upside was that their education would be at the Dominican Convent School.

Mother Superior showed us their dormitories, which had a happy vibe. Each girl had a counterpane in the colour of her choice, and a cubicle that could be decorated to reflect their individual personality. We met Sister Edith, a young nun from Germany, Fay's house mother. Plans were made to have Fay and Gail with us at Domboshawa for the following week-end and the Christmas school holidays, too.

Woohoo!

Perhaps this was not the wisest decision, as Brian had been transferred to Goromonzi High School and moving day was 11 January. How would the girls cope with another removal upheaval? But we did not want them to spend the holidays with another family and become attached to anyone but us. They settled back into their old room happily and helped with the packing.

# NINE

# A Time to Love

## Winds of Change

The winds of change were blowing through colonial Africa in 1964, and our move to Goromonzi was part of that change. The government decision to close Domboshawa Technical Training Institute at the end of 1963 caused anxiety among both staff and students. We were still reeling from the break-up of The Federation, and now jobs were on the line. Places were found for students at other colleges, but there were no plans to open another training facility. Our colleagues, who had become our friends, would be scattered. Three families made the decision to return to their UK roots; others focussed on securing teaching posts around the country.

Brian was offered a position as teacher of woodwork and technical drawing at Goromonzi High School, a boarding school in a farming area, twenty-five miles from the city and five miles from the nearest petrol station and post office. He would be a teacher at an academic school, not a trade instructor—a different career path opening for him. He recognised the opportunity to upgrade his qualifications, converting his City and Guilds building diploma into an academic teaching certificate.

It sounded good, but would he be able to commit to years of study? And would all those academics accept him, a former tradesman, as an equal? He earnestly prayed for guidance to make the right decision. There was no writing in the sky, but Brian was convinced that God was directing him into the career he had always wanted. So, the offer was accepted, and we packed up our belongings and made the move in January 1964, misgivings and all!

Initially, I'd been anxious about the change too. But from the very first week, we were made welcome, both on campus and in the surrounding farming area. The local postmaster gifted a bicycle, for Fay and Gail, which they shared (one on the pillion!), riding round with their new friends Mary-Pat and Michael. There was a closeness among the residential staff of Goromonzi High School, almost a family feeling and no racial divide. I felt socially inadequate when mixing with people whose education level was so much higher than my own and would become embarrassed and tongue-tied. Gill—a teacher herself before her first son was born and now pregnant with baby number two— welcomed and befriended me;. A smiley Welsh girl with a lilt to her voice and a warm, fun-loving personality, Gill was a real blessing.

In Gill I recognised an intellect I lacked, and I decided to do something about that. The school library was extensive and available to students, staff, and families—a great resource to make up for those years, when I could have been studying at university. If a book was mentioned at a staff social gathering I would make a mental note and ferret it out for my reading material. Classics skipped over at school were revisited and modern authors discovered. This was a season of growth for me and confidence gained; I even learned to play bridge.

Goromonzi was where we became a proper family. Craig and Ann were both born while we were living there; each arrival was a miracle in its own way.

## First Miracle

The night of Wednesday 17 June 1964 is forever etched in my memory. We'd spent the afternoon in town, carpooled to save petrol, and accepted Gill's invitation to dinner. After dinner there was a game of bridge—colleague Graham B joining us for coffee and post-mortem! Brian and I headed home very late.

"Goodnight! Goodnight!"

"Watch the step. Do you want a torch?"

"Thanks for a lovely dinner, great evening, pity about that four no trumps"

"Keep your voices down. It's after eleven."

"Sorry. See you tomorrow."

"Goodnight! Goodnight!

The calls and laughter followed us down the path into the road that led from their house, around the corner, and up the sanitary lane to the back of our house. The road was just a track—two ruts with a hummock of grass between—making progress in the dark a slow business; we linked arms. The moonlight played on the mulberry trees lining the lane and shadowed the gap leading into the back garden of the house that had been our home for the past six months. We followed the path around to the veranda.

The stark light above our front door highlighted a note stuck onto the glass. Intrigued, Brian peeled off the sticky tape and opened the envelope. He handed it to me without a word.

The note read, in Ollie's scrawl:

Phone Mrs S, social welfare urgently. She has
called three times! They have a baby boy—
need to know if you want him. I told them
*yes*! Don't give him to anyone else. Hope
you do want him. My three are enough!
Congratulations, Mum and Dad.

We stood staring at each other, the front door still closed.
Our prayers had been answered, the waiting time shortened.
All those tests, treatments, operations, disappointments, and
heartbreak when it seemed babies were not for us—how we
had longed for this day!

It seemed a lifetime ago that we had completed application
forms to adopt a baby; in fact, it was two and a half years.
The wait time was a minimum of three years, possibly five we .
had been told by our officer, the lovely Mrs S. She had made
numerous visits, announced and unannounced, checking on
our lifestyle, getting to know us and the type of parents we
would be.

In April, she had dropped in with the wonderful news
that we could now consider ourselves "pregnant". We had
progressed onto the short list. Believing we had nine months
before becoming parents, I had agreed to be relief domestic
science teacher for a term, filling a gap until the new teacher
arrived from the United Kingdom in August. But that night,
the ramifications of time juggling around work and baby did
not enter my head.

Our baby boy had arrived!

There was no telephone in our home, and the school offices
were closed until the following morning, so we could only try
to get some sleep—possibly the last for a while with a new
baby. The nursery was ready for our long-awaited child, the
drawers filled with clothes mostly made by me. The walls were

washed in a pretty pale blue with white woodwork and blue curtains with an animal pattern; there was a change table made by Brian and a lovely crib, also made by Brian and trimmed by me in white spotted voile. I packed a small suitcase, carefully choosing the outfit to bring home our son—a white Viyella nightie, lace trimmed and embroidered with bluebells (this was before the days of Babygro), a blue cross over jersey with matching booties. Vest and nappies went into the bag too, along with a wrapping blanket in blue, pink, and white floral and a lovely circular shawl knitted with love and many prayers by a would-be mum.

Sleep didn't come. I planned our trip to Bulawayo to collect our son; should we go by train tomorrow night or start the six-hour journey by road the following morning? It was usual for babies born in Mashonaland to be placed for adoption with parents in Matabeleland and vice versa. My mind did flick flacks as I mentally sorted clothes to pack for myself and Brian. I hardly slept a wink.

Brian was on roll call duty at seven thirty, so we walked down to the school together. I hung around the empty office, anxious and agitated, waiting until the dot of eight, when I dialled the number and heard Mrs S's voice. "Is that you, Marie?"

"Yes, yes it's me," I spluttered. "We were out until late last night and didn't get the message till we got home. Is it true? We have a baby?"

She laughed "Yes it's true. You are a mummy, and Brian's a daddy"

I learned that we had been chosen to be the parents of a baby boy, ten days old weighing eight pounds two ounces.

"Can you be here at the office with his clothes by nine o'clock?" she asked.

"When, which day?" I replied.

"Today!" she almost shouted back.

My mind went into overdrive. An hour! There would need to be some low flying. No time for a call to my mum and dad. Classes were organised with stand-in teachers for the day, and we leapt into the car. Good thinking to have packed the baby bag last night.

An empty parking place directly opposite the building beckoned; we parked and dashed across the road. The rickety old lift with metal latticed gate was waiting in the foyer to jerk and wobble us up to the fourth floor. The office door was ajar, revealing the beaming faces of staff waiting with a tangible sense of anticipation. These caring people witnessed so much hurt and heartache in their chosen careers, walking alongside young women making agonising decisions. We were the other side of the coin—a young couple eager and longing to be parents.

Mrs S took just a few minutes to tell us how we had jumped to the top of the list. There were eight couples ahead of us. Some wanted girls. Another was abroad on leave. And others were not a good background match. She took the clothes bag, telling us, "Go and get a cup of tea," as she headed towards the Lady Chancellor Maternity Home.

When we walked out onto the pavement to cross the road, a traffic warden was in the act of writing out a parking ticket. In our haste, we had forgotten to feed the meter!

Our friends Hope and Charlie lived nearby, so we headed there to share the news with them and phone my mum. Their son Tony was Brian's best buddy and best man at our wedding. They had laughed and cried with us over our disappointments in trying to have a baby. My mum, in Sinoia, cried with joy to be a grandma at last! Plans were made for them to drive to Goromonzi on Saturday; they would meet their first grandchild in two days.

His name had already been chosen, Craig Edward. We wanted a saint's name for our son, and the Gaelic Craig means the same as Peter, the Rock. Edward after his daddy, Brian's middle name. And that day, we added Paul. My mother assumed Paul was for my brother who died at birth, but there was another reason. Collection date was 18 June, Paul McCartney's birthday, and Brian and I were avid Beatles fans! Now I recognise the anointed faith of the Apostle Paul, but then …

The front office was empty when we returned. My stomach was a knot of nervousness, mixed with anticipation as the bell dinged. Where was everyone? Were they all cooing and cuddling our baby! The receptionist showed us into the small office where Mrs S was holding a bundle wrapped in my hand-knitted shawl. She placed our son into my arms.

Brian and I stood looking into the beautiful face of our sleeping baby; at last, we were parents! I wanted to go home quickly, just us. But there were things to be said, papers to be signed, and feeding details to be made aware of. A bottle of formula had been made up at the maternity home, and I fed Craig his first feed as my son. When we finally headed home to Goromonzi, I sat in the front seat holding my baby, unheard of now. No seat belts, but I am sure there were angels around that car!

The weeks after Craig's arrival were a mix of highs and lows. Highs were when I held him, sang to him, marvelled at our son. Lows were when he cried at night, from colic and I did not know why. The school timetable was adjusted so I could have a feeding break from ten until eleven. He was such a "good" baby, sleeping in his pram while I was busy with the class. I agreed to carry on teaching despite the increase in stress levels, until the students sat their mock exams in July; the girls were thrilled to have a baby parked on the veranda.

## Legally Ours!

The adoption hearing took place on 12 August in the Salisbury(now Harare) Magistrates Court. The Magistrate was at the head of the table, with me to his left, holding a fractious baby. When the pages of the document were turned, all Craig's birth details appeared before my eyes. I tried to look away—this is forbidden information, to be hidden by law. When the magistrate caught my eye, he winked. Did he intend me to see this information? The hearing was over in less than half an hour, and Craig was now legally our son.

On the Sunday after the adoption hearing when he legally became our son, 16 August1964, Craig was presented for infant baptism at St Mark's Church, Ruwa. Brian had rejected Christian Science relatively quickly and returned to worshipping God at our local Anglican church. Vows were made on his behalf by Craig's godparents Myrna, Gideon, my cousin Graham,and by Brian and me. As I pray now for my adult son, I stand on the truth that Craig was dedicated to Jesus at eight weeks old.

Fay and Gail, now ten and eight, spent alternate weekends with us and became big sisters. Our names were back on the list for baby number two, an expected wait of three or more years.

# TEN

# A Time for Even More Loving

## UDI

The years of 1964 and 1965 saw political upheaval in Southern Rhodesia. Sabres had been rattling since the break-up of the federation, but my life each day was so focussed on being a new mum, I hardly noticed the build-up of political tension.

Then the bubble burst when Ian Smith declared Rhodesia's unilateral independence from Britain, and uncertainty shrouded our lives—not quite fear but pretty close! Northern Rhodesia and Nyasaland had become Zambia and Malawi respectively, but the Southern Rhodesian government would not accept universal adult suffrage without understanding, so no independent status was granted by Britain. Discussions on the Goromonzi campus around politics had been deep and often heated; hopes were raised with each round of talks but when Harold Wilson and Ian Smith failed once again to come to an agreement, rumours of impending UDI were rife.

On 11 November, Brian and I tuned into the radio to listen to an important speech by the Prime Minister. The lengthy proclamation covered issues and attitudes, ending with:

Now therefore, we the Government of Rhodesia, in humble submission to Almighty God who controls the destinies of nations, conscious that the people of Rhodesia have always shown unswerving loyalty and devotion to Her Majesty the Queen and earnestly praying that we and the people of Rhodesia will not be hindered in our determination to continue exercising our undoubted right to demonstrate the same loyalty and devotion, and seeking to promote the common good so that the dignity and freedom of all men may be assured, Do, By This Proclamation, adopt, enact and give to the people of Rhodesia, the Constitution annexed hereto.

What did that all mean? I found the speech confusing to say the least. Maybe if the "constitution annexed hereto" had been read out, I would have known what was happening. Ian Smith had not said, "I declare UDI."

When he ended his speech with the words, "God save the queen," there was a stunned silence at our table.

"Has he done it?" I asked.

"I think so, but I'm not sure," said Brian.

We sat in silence trying to take it all in.

Had it actually happened? What would it mean for us?

At that moment, we heard the revving of a car and the sound of tyres skidding on the dirt road, as our avidly anti-Smith colleague, Jimmy E sped out of the campus and headed towards his Brit cronies in town. We knew! It *had* happened. Rhodesia was now no longer part of Britain!

Politics had never been high on our list of interests or

priorities, but our conversations now included questions like, "Will our British passports be renewed?" and, "Should we become Rhodesian citizens and swear allegiance to Smith's government?" We said things like, "This is the country we live in and that provides our livelihood! So, we should be citizens." And we wondered out loud, "Should we emigrate to Canada?" The latter was an attractive option but it wasn't going to happen, with both sets of parents living in Rhodesia. It was a time of uncertainty, vulnerability, and fear of the unknown future

I have shared this, not for the political content but as a background to what happened next.

## Another Miracle

While my mind was on these matters of magnitude, the miracle happened—the miracle we'd prayed for over the past seven years! My period was three weeks late before I woke up to the fact that I could be pregnant. A urine sample was sent to the laboratory for a pregnancy test; over-the-counter test kits were not available in 1965. An appointment was made with my gynaecologist for the result. Just a confirmation. I was sure! This was *it*. I was already experiencing morning sickness.

Mr C told me, "The rabbit has died!"

Did the rabbit ever actually die? Probably not. But there were obvious changes if the donor was pregnant. And I *was*.

The due date was calculated to be 11 August, nine months to the day after UDI.

Christmas that year was full of joy. My mum and dad drove in for lunch on Christmas Eve to share the excitement en route to an Nyanga holiday with friends. We were spending Christmas with Brian's folks and the rest of the Bishop clan.

Craig was given his first car (at 18 months) by Granny and Grandpa Bishop—a red pedal car. Mum B knitted some gorgeous bootees "for the one not here yet". The whole family was excited.

The only drawback was the constant sickness, worse in the evening when I needed to prepare dinner. And instead of stopping after the first trimester, it went on for the entire pregnancy. I walked into the delivery room carrying a Petri dish!

## D-Day

Friday 29 July was a lovely warm day—an ideal drying day, so I did two big loads of washing and was hanging out the second load when I heard Brian's, "Helloooo." It was morning tea break at school; my mother had telephoned from Sinoia. She had woken early that morning feeling sure today was the day, even though it was still two weeks from the due date! Mum wanted to know if I was having pains, twinges, anything.

Brian called her back and said, "Nothing happening. She's hanging out the washing."

But by the time Brian came home for lunch, I was not so sure.

"My lunch is in the oven," I said. "You and Craig go ahead. I just want to stretch out a bit and check on this backache."

The pain in my back was quite strong and seemed to be stopping and starting. I timed the pains—coming regularly every ten minutes. Could it be? No one had told me contractions could be in the back!

When I told Brian I thought the "backache" was labour pains, he went into overdrive. Headed to school without finishing his dinner, classes to sort out, needed to phone sister

Rosemary who would look after Craig. The call back to Mum could be done from Rosemary's. We needed to get on the road to the maternity home twenty-five miles away ASAP!

The plan was to drop me off at the Lady Chancellor for examination and assessment, and Brian would then deliver Craig and be back. The time was nearly three when I was booked in, and Brian was back again before four. He was a tower of strength, filling hot water bottles, rubbing my back, and timing contractions.

All went according to plan. Mr Cameron had two babies on the go at the same time, so he moved between the two rooms checking our progress and making it a race between the mums. Finally, time to go to the delivery room, and Brian walked with me to the door, still carrying a Petri dish for morning sickness. No husbands were allowed at deliveries in 1966, so he returned to the waiting room. Within half an hour, at ten minutes to seven, our beautiful daughter was born weighing seven pounds, ten ounces. Brian was invited back into the room and was able to hold our precious girl while the staff finished tidying me up.

Brian had called Mum and Dad from Rosemary's, and they made the 100-kilometre drive from Sinoia in time to hear that they had a granddaughter. No visitors to new mums either in 1966, so they collected Craig from Rosemary's and headed back to Goromonzi. Brian stayed with me until I was transferred to the ward and baby Elisabeth Ann to the nursery. He went home to a meal cooked by Granny, but I was starving, having missed lunch and dinner! The hospital breakfast of porridge and eggs on toast next morning tasted like a banquet.

The name we had originally chosen for our longed-for daughter was Catherine Elisabeth, but friend Tiffy had called her number three daughter Catherine. Brian was adamant we could not use the same name. We kept Elisabeth, my name and my mother's and added Ann, Elisabeth Ann. I liked the Welsh short form Bethan. But Bethan Bishop did not flow well, so she became Ann. This means Grace, perfect for our beautiful baby girl.

She was a placid baby from day one; in fact she was five days old before I heard her cry properly. I was in the bathroom when the babies were brought for feeding, and as I approached my cubicle, I heard a strange sound. My baby girl had been placed on my bed and she was crying for food—or her mummy!

The nursing staff on level one of the Lady Chancellor were intrigued I was classed as a primipara but had an older child. When they heard about Craig's adoption, the pieces were put together, dates checked, and they knew he was "their baby". He was the one they had cared for, cuddled, and loved for ten days after his birth mother had left the hospital and while parents were selected. They wanted to see their "Markie" again. So, Brian and my mum brought Craig to the hospital grounds, and they were all able to see their baby as a confident two-year-old boy, now a big brother.

Mum stayed and cared for Brian and Craig for the week I was in hospital. Dad planned to spend the weekend at Goromonzi and meet his new granddaughter. Brian collected me from hospital Friday morning, and we drove home, carrycot on the back seat 1960s style.

Craig came running to the car; he gave me a quick hug and then peered into the back of the car commanding, "Get it out."

He ran indoors, ahead of us, seating himself in the rocking chair, arms out. I placed the sleeping baby into his arms, while Brian grabbed the camera. Craig held his week-old sister tightly, gently kissing the top of her head. She opened her eyes. Was that a smile?

It was the start of their sibling relationship.

# ELEVEN

# A Time to Embrace Change

## Country Life

Raising children on Goromonzi school campus was the ideal way to go. Most of the staff had families, so there was always company for the children. There were tennis courts, along with a swimming pool at both the school and the sports club up the road. Summer Island offered riding lessons for children from 4 years old, although Ann had her first ride at 3. Those early days were halcyon days. Craig enjoyed visiting our friend's farm to play with classmates Maureen and Ian and watch dehorning and branding processes. Was this the start of his love for agriculture, which is his life now?

The "local" primary school at Ruwa, fifteen miles away, provided education for the first three years, KG 1 and 2 and standard 1. We registered Craig there with the rest of the Goromonzi kids. School was really an extension of play time. They travelled with the same friends who they rode horses or played with at the club. Mothers formed a carpool, meeting at collection points and taking turns fetching and carrying the children.

Teacher Jean C somehow managed to discipline and teach forty plus children of different ages and abilities, with only one assistant. What a legend! All three age groups were in one large room, divided into desk lines. The lines were flexible enough to separate noisy friends, like Craig and Adam. Mrs C made school fun—never any "don't want to go" days.

But we knew important decisions would need to be made before Craig reached the end of the standard 1 year. The farming community had no option other than sending their children to boarding school, but we wanted ours at home with us. This would mean moving closer to the city and day schools, leaving behind the country life we had grown to love.

## Plans to Transfer to City Life

We saw this as the right time to buy a house instead of renting. A new suburb called Ashdown Park was opening up. Prices were affordable, and my cousin Tony and his family were moving to Salisbury from Sinoia. We liked the idea of the cousins growing up together, so went to investigate. The houses were small. They were well-designed but on small pieces of land and very close to neighbours. They were a far cry from the rambling farmhouses and distant vistas we'd become accustomed to over the past twelve years.

Enter Brian, the dreamer, declaring he had "always dreamed" of building his own house! He suggested we buy a plot, and he would draw up plans and do much of the work himself. We looked at land for sale in the northern suburbs, great sections close to good schools, but way out of our price range. Full payment was required before building started, and there were clauses dictating start and finish times. As owner builders we could not comply.

As his latest dream appeared to be moving out of reach, Brian prayed for direction. Should we settle for the smaller house on a small section in Ashdown Park? Look for a cottage on an acre of land, needing repair and going cheap? Or rent? He drove around the northern suburbs on free days searching for a piece of land we could afford. On one reccy, he discovered a large section of land between Borrowdale and Helensvale pegged out for plots. There was no signage, but it looked remarkably like a new subdivision. Next stop, the Round House council building, where an official confirmed it was to be a new suburb called Greystone Park and handed Brian a list of sections, sizes, and prices.

This area was outside the city limits, so there would be no municipal services, no rates, just an annual road tax, septic tanks instead of piped sewage, and no rubbish collection. We had lived in the sticks for twelve years, so were not fazed by a rubbish pit in the garden! Best of all, the deposit was only 10 per cent, with the balance payable over three years and no building time clauses. It was a perfect answer to prayer.

Each weekend, we drove through the new suburb, price lists in hand, looking at plots. Initially, there was no sense of urgency. But as we moved at a leisurely pace, two things happened—Greystone Park was rapidly gaining popularity, and the prices were increasing. Each time we called the council to secure a plot of our choice, someone else had beaten us to it. Now the search became urgent. This could be our last chance; we could miss out!

We found a plot we both liked. It was an acre of gently sloping ground, in a cul-de-sac bordered by a stream leading to an open vlei at the bottom of the garden. There were houses on either side, one a home to a young family. This was the one! We could just scrape together the 10 per cent of the asking price.

But when Brian telephoned to secure the plot the price had been increased. We needed more for the deposit.

Our spirits sank again. Our neighbours Hein and Henny had been following the saga with us, and when they saw our disappointment, Hein offered to lend the difference with the proviso that it must be paid back within nine months, as this was from their savings for return fares to their home in Holland. Alleluia, what a blessing those friends were! The deposit was paid the next day. We were land owners. Brian enjoyed telling people that he had bought our land with Dutch aid.

## Building the House at Number 8

The next stage was the actual house. Brian drew plans and priced them and then scaled them down and priced them— again and again. The Building Society loan was calculated on Brian's earnings as a teacher; I was a full-time Mum and not contributing to the family income, so our budget was restricted to the amount we could borrow, £10,000. We continued to make monthly payments against the land loan, and when we were ready to start building, this was refunded into our account, an invaluable start-up to use for materials.

The foundations were dug, and the concrete slab laid by Brian. The work was checked by the building inspector, who gave the okay, and the first tranche of the loan was transferred, enabling brick layers to be employed. Our house was underway! Brian travelled the twenty-five miles from Goromonzi every second day to check progress and spent each weekend working at the site. He camped on site whilst constructing the roof trusses—all done by hand in one long weekend. That night, his arm was still sawing as he slept!

My cousins moved into their new completed house just as

we started building. There were times when we wondered if we had made the right decision; for the same money, we could be already housed in a completed home, instead of facing months of hard work. But we were zoned for the schools of our choice, and we would have our custom designed home eventually, with a large garden.

Brian made all the external hardwood window frames and doors, and the pine ceilings were a feature. My contribution initially was starting to terrace the acre of sloping garden. As the building progressed, I took on painting the inside walls and laying mosaic tiling in the two showers. I learned the hard way, skinning my fingers when working without gloves and having to explain why I had bloody hands when attending a staff cocktail party at Brian's school!

## New Home

Occupancy was set for the September school holidays. But on moving in day, the electrician had not finished in time to have his work signed off by the building inspector! There was no power, no lights or stove, only candles, a Primus, and cold showers until the power could be switched on.

Brian was very despondent when he delivered the first load of furniture and his family to the unfinished home. The bulk of construction was completed, but many finishing touches still to be done. Despite the end being really close, he felt a sense of failure. The painting in the third bedroom was unfinished, and lighting was still to be added, so all extra furniture and boxes were put into that room. This would be the guest room initially and eventually Craig's room. Meanwhile, both children shared the middle room with bunk beds.

The parquet floors all needed sealing, which would be my

job once Brian was back at work. But, on moving day, my main task was to create an oasis of comfort! A brightly coloured Axminster carpet went down in the dining room, covering most of the unsealed floor. The sideboard was positioned with a camping light on it, wild flowers from the garden were placed on the dining table, and two easy chairs with a coffee table between effectively shielded the unfinished drinks cupboard from view.

When Brian arrived back with the final load of furniture, his face lit up, and his spirits lifted at the sight of an orderly, attractive, relaxing, small living area and the kettle boiling in the kitchen on our camping stove, Our new home was coming together! Dinner that night was at the drive-in, cooking without electricity too big a challenge for tired parents. For Craig and Ann, country kids, this was a special family celebration treat. We all fell into bed exhausted.

Early next morning, we were woken by the sun streaming into our bedroom, showcasing the small developed area of garden. Pelmets were one of the finishing touches waiting to happen, so no curtains were hung on the large floor-to-ceiling windows. The people and cars on the road bordering the vlei were clearly visible to us—so we were also on display! It was like sleeping in a shop window. We quickly dressed and were ready to go.

The electricity was turned on later that day as scheduled, and Brian could use power tools to get onto finishing the house.

## Overdraught

By Christmas, our dream home was becoming a reality, layer by layer as the remaining tasks were completed. The garden was taking shape, and it felt like home. The fly in the ointment was the huge overdraft of £2,000!

We needed more income to clear the debt; it was time for me to look for a mornings-only job "just until the overdraft was paid". My wise mother-in-law said the equivalent of the Kiwi, "Yeah right." She prophesied this would be "the thin end of the wedge", and I would be working for the rest of my life.

I telephoned a doctor's surgery who was advertising for a mornings-only cashier/receptionist come trainee practice nurse, twenty-five hours weekly. An interview was arranged and successful, and I started with Drs Joe and Gerry in February 1971, believing it would be temporary until the overdraught cleared. That temporary work lasted for ten years.

My mum-in-law was right!

# TWELVE

# A Time to Laugh and
# a Time to Weep

*May the favour of the Lord our God rest
upon us; establish the work of our hands
for us – yes, establish the work of our hands.*
**—Psalms 90:17 (NIV)**

## Work for my hands

I had enjoyed my life as a full-time stay-at-home mum. But, when that overdraught jettisoned me out of my comfort zone, skills that had lain dormant for ten years emerged. Today's school leavers are told that they can expect at least six careers over their working life. I can certainly count six or more changes of direction in my own life, each requiring different skills.

During those years as a homemaker, my sewing skills came to the fore, creating clothes for myself and the children. Ann was seven before knowing the excitement of trying on and choosing a dress in a shop, for Uncle Bill's wedding! Neighbours requested alterations and repairs, providing spending money. But now we needed an increased monthly income to clear the overdraft with our bank, not just spending money. Both children were at school; it was time to resuscitate my office skills.

I had never planned to be what my dad would call an "office wallah". As a young girl, my dream career had been nursing. During fourth form at school, I'd volunteered as a cadet nurse at the local hospital in Garston, doing menial tasks. This gave me insight into hospital work at age fifteen, until I could register for SRN training at eighteen. Then came the upheaval of the family moving to Rhodesia. Cadet nursing was not on offer in Rhodesia, so I applied for SRN training. There was a long waiting list for the Salisbury training school, and when a place was eventually offered four years later, I was engaged to Brian and planning my wedding. So, I turned away from that dream and focussed on becoming a good "office wallah".

The years with Drs Joe and Gerry also gave me basic nursing knowledge, as I stood in for the "nurses" during leave. In fact, as neither of the practice nurses were SRNs, the doctors, administered injections, took patients' blood pressure, and changed dressings. Dr Joe delighted in saying he preferred trained stooges to trained sisters, who would probably try to control him. The trained stooges manned the phones, made appointments, sterilised instruments, prepared Petri dishes for various procedures, and held patients' hands as they were stitched or injected. The reality was, even if I had trained as a nurse, motherhood would have intervened, and I would have sought work as a practice nurse. So, I had just missed the middle bit. I loved my work at the surgery and would have stayed forever—had it not been for a new development.

## Another Dream

Another of Brian's dreams began to surface. This was a "no-time frame dream", on the back burner, a "someday" dream. But it surfaced during the construction of a new shopping complex in the Avenues, close to the doctor's surgery. The dream was for a hardware shop, out of which Brian could do home maintenance and some building.

Our interest was registered with the agent, and we did the math. We had some savings, not a lot of money, so would be undercapitalised. But starting from scratch, with no goodwill payment required, we believed could do this on a shoestring! The progress on the building site was painfully slow. Completion date had been shifted from late 1979 to the following year. We felt as though we were marking time.

With the precious gift of hindsight, I can now see that, far from marking time, God was at work, loosening ties, shaking, and redirecting our lives.

## Spiritual Shake-Ups

Brian had not pursued Christian Science after we left Domboshawa. During our time at Goromonzi, the children were christened at St Mark's, and Brian returned to Anglican worship. When we moved to Greystone Park, he regularly attended evensong; he was still questioning, and searching for answers, but his faith was being restored. There was a chasm between us spiritually, which became the elephant in our lives. He tried to share his faith with me, but I thought I was managing well without God, no change needed. He tried to share his faith with our friends, too. One of our friends nicknamed Brian a "God-botherer", and he accepted this as a compliment!

My face had been turned away from God for almost ten years. During that time, I was doing what most of our friends were doing—enjoying whatever life offered, taking all the blessings as my right, my due. The children were making good progress at school. We each had jobs we enjoyed. Brian was teaching at a prestigious boys' school, and I loved my work at the surgery. Weekends were usually spent with friends either out at the fisheries with Sue and Brian or with "the Hammies".

I felt good about making my own decisions, no handbrakes, no yardstick for measuring whether those decisions were right or wrong. Some of those decisions were wrong, extremely wrong and could have ruined our family, but for God's restraining hand, which held me in check.

The Rhodesian Civil War, the Second Chimurenga, was raging, and Brian was called up for army duties during school holidays. Curfews meant lonely nights after the children were in bed. My Godless life may have looked good on the surface, but there was a void deep down. I may have been firing well on two cylinders, body and soul, but the third cylinder, spirit, was not firing at all. And that meant our children were experiencing spiritual deprivation. I had defaulted on the vows I'd made at their christenings. No regular church or Sunday school attendance. Can that be classed as spiritual abuse?

On Easter Sunday, I woke with a conviction that we needed to go to Church, so we headed off to Borrowdale Anglican Church for their nine thirty service—only to discover the start time was actually nine fifteen, and the service was well under way. Too embarrassed to push into the crowded church, we drove to another local church, Kingsmead. But their service also started at nine fifteen, and that little chapel was bursting at the seams!

Deflated, we went home, toasted hot cross buns, and ate chocolate eggs with the rest of the pagan world.

I know now that God *never* takes His hand off His children even when we turn away from Him. And this was the start of a series of shake-ups in our lives.

## Joy and Despair

In August, I knew something was happening to me, physically. Dr Joe confirmed I was not experiencing early menopause at thirty-five but, rather, that I was pregnant. No treatment, no special efforts. Out of the blue, pregnant! Craig and Ann, now ten and eight, were over the moon excited to hear they would have a baby sister or brother in April next year. Every conversation turned to "the baby". Names were discussed. Xavier was a favourite of Craig's. Brian was convinced we would have a boy and wanted to name him Esau, but James— my dad's middle name—resonated with me.

Gynaecologist Mr C was delighted too; he had predicted from our first consultation that I would have babies "eventually", citing a forty-year-old patient as evidence—not at all reassuring for a twenty-two-year-old! But he was right, and I was pregnant for the second time. He assured me at every visit that everything was progressing according to plan. This was before scans, but I heard the baby's heart beating strongly. No sickness, so maybe a boy this time.

Then, early on Monday morning when he was at fourteen weeks gestation, baby James dropped into my hand as I visited the bathroom. No pain, no bleeding, just a perfectly formed little person, expelled from my womb without any warning! I was stunned, all feelings frozen in that moment. Mr C could give no clue what had caused the miscarriage of this much loved and longed-for baby.

Years later, I discovered the possible cause, when reading a report by another gynaecologist of another miscarriage, caused by unintentionally inhaling malathion while using it in the garden. Then I remembered using a chemical in our garden on that fateful Sunday—pouring it into the holes of crickets that were keeping us awake at night. The smell was so strong we all went to sister Rosemary's for afternoon tea! My gardening zeal had killed my baby. Fortunately, I did not know that then. The loss was enough to bear without any added guilt.

I can still recall that emptiness when I returned home on Monday night after the D and C. Ann and Craig piled onto the bed with me—cuddling in close. They were confused and fearful, not understanding what had happened. Nor did I at that time. I just felt as though I was in limbo, no idea what to do next. Then depression hit me, which was isolating. I was far from God during those wilderness years. But someone must have been praying, because somehow, I came through it all without dependence on pills. It was a month before I could physically or emotionally face returning to work. And the grieving continued long after.

After Christmas, we decided to join our friends the Hammies on holiday in Durban in an attempt to get back to normal. The journey was a nightmare. Four people and luggage squashed into the Karmann Ghia for a 1,200-mile journey! But the holiday was a relaxing bonding time for our family, a time of healing. The change of pace and activity did shift some of my grief, and we all enjoyed fun on the beaches with our combined four children, along with eating out, movies, and ice skating.

## Grief

Refreshed and restored, we headed home, intending to spend a night with my parents in Fort Victoria, not knowing another heartache awaited us. When we arrived at their home around six thirty, there was a casserole in the oven, but the flat was empty, no message on the door. Where could they be? Maybe with neighbours next door.

"Not here," they told us "An ambulance came about an hour ago and took Les to hospital on a stretcher. Betty said he was bringing up blood."

We piled back into the car and headed to the hospital. Mum was in the waiting room looking anxious and dissolved into tears at the sight of us. Dad had a perforated stomach ulcer and was in surgery. Brian took the children back to the flat to settle for the night. I stayed with Mum, found us cups of tea, and we settled down for a long wait. Dad had suffered with rheumatoid arthritis for over ten years, needing medication for mobility and pain relief. This medication, over an extended period, and probably taken with alcohol, had caused an ulcer in his stomach, which had perforated. He was in the operating theatre for six hours.

This initial procedure appeared to be a success, but two days later, the wound burst open, invoking screams of excruciating agony, as the stomach acids spread over the raw internal wounds. Cortisone, which had been added to Dad's medication, had thinned his body tissues, and the surgical wounds were not healing. The surgeon planned to operate again when he was strong enough to survive a second operation. Meanwhile, Dad's screams and obvious agony were heart-wrenching.

My thought was to go ahead with the second operation now. What did it matter if he died on the operating table if he was going to die anyway? My mother stood firmly against this; her faith was steady and strong throughout. She believed there was a right time for my father to die, God's timing, not to be hastened along. She sat by him constantly, holding his hand and praying. The pain was gradually brought under control, and the doctor and nurses focused on building his strength for another operation.

## Waiting in Hope

Once Dad was stable, we headed home to Salisbury so Brian and the children could start the new term. I went back to work during the week and made the road trip to Fort Victoria at weekends—four hours each way—ignoring the guerrilla war.

This was at the time when I still had my back turned away from God, so, although I spent time with my father, I was not praying for his healing. Mum would have been praying non-stop. I wonder if Dad did too, in his later years? I had never known him to pray—he had been a scoffer as long as I could remember. Mum's church involvement had often been the focus of his jokes.

He had a keen quick wit, the dry sense of humour common to Liverpudlians, a big man, fun to be with. He kept his family and friends in fits of laughter with his jokes and anecdotes, unless you were the butt of his humour.

My mother was a member of Fort Victoria Wesleyan Methodist Church, attending Sunday service regularly, and she occasionally persuaded Dad to go with her. He was certainly not scoffing as he lay in his hospital bed, in pain and growing weaker. Peter W was the new young minister at Mum's church—his first church ministry. He visited Dad every day and spent time talking to him.

When I arrived at the hospital on the Friday afternoon, just hours before he died, Dad opened his eyes and whispered to me, "I'm not going to make it, love." He closed his eyes and appeared to be sleeping but then opened them again and reached out his hand. "I've made my peace with God." From my own perspective, far from God, that meant absolutely nothing. Just words.

Peter W took the funeral service and told the congregation how Dad had turned back to God during his dying days. But again, this did not resonate with me. I did not question or ask for more detail, just let my dad go.

I focussed on supporting Mum.

# THIRTEEN

# A Time to Die

The ring on our party line jolted me from semi sleep—*tring, tring tring; trrrring, trrrring, trrrring*—three shorts, three longs; that's us!

I reached the hall and the phone at the end of the next ring, glancing at the clock in the lounge—5.25 p.m. Brian should be home with the kids by now; he must have stopped at the supermarket.

I spoke into the handset. "8874626"

The line crackled—hissing over the airwaves—a faint voice in the distance. "Is that you, love? Marie? Is that you?" I heard the quavery voice of my Auntie Glad.

She had always been a bit deaf—not really deaf like Auntie Nance but hard of hearing. Now the distance and the party line made for scrappy communication.

"It's your Mum, pet," she called out. "She is poorly—very poorly."

"What's wrong?" I shouted back.

"She took sick when we got back from Devon," Auntie Glad shouted down the line. "We thought it was too many Devonshire teas. The doctor put her in hospital for observation;

he says she's worse now. She is very poorly, love. You should come."

"How poorly? Is she really ill?"

*Crackle hiss, crackle hiss*, down the party line.

"I can't hear you Marie; I'll get Uncle Les to call later."

The phone went dead. I stood there looking at the wall. What did *poorly* mean?

## Mum's Holiday

My mother, Betty, had been having her *once-in-a-lifetime* holiday in the United Kingdom with her family since May. Betty and Les had shared holidays with brother Les and Glad, in the United Kingdom and Zimbabwe. But as arthritis became disfiguring and movement more painful, Dad would not commit to another holiday. After he died, her first priority was overseeing the completion of the cottage they had started, their dream home for retirement. She turned down our suggestion to add a granny flat onto our house and moved to Penhalonga alone, determined to make a new life in that picturesque village, near to friends Marge and Fred.

Next was the plan for a holiday to England visiting family there. This plan was almost derailed in December when Mum discovered a lump in her breast, which was diagnosed as breast dancer. She forged ahead stoically, with surgery and radiotherapy and was given the all-clear by the oncologist— told to go and enjoy her holiday, and they would discuss further treatment when she returned.

How could I be so dumb? I worked for a doctor—read patients' reports. I should have known Dr M was telling her to enjoy what time was left—carpe diem! Did Mum keep that knowledge to herself to protect me?

## Parting

We'd waved her off at the airport. Her Siamese cat, Tora, was now well settled in with our menagerie. The postcards came thick and fast—lovely times shared with her oldest and best friend Irene; Uncle Eric became the chauffeur, and they became two girls again. Her two older sisters Nance and Lily were in their element. Mum had been "their baby" in 1914. Now they were just three sisters! They all sent postcards sharing the fun they were having reconnecting with each other, visiting places where memories had been made and making new ones.

And now this phone call—she was poorly, whatever *poorly* meant.

Uncle Les phoned at seven thirty that evening. He said my lovely mummy was dying. The sickness was not related to Devonshire teas but cancer, which had spread to her brain and was causing the vomiting. Uncle Les had already called my brothers, Tony and Stuart, and they were both preparing to fly to the United Kingdom. He said I should come too.

## Decisions

I stood in the hall, phone in hand, shivering, stunned.

Brian led me back to bed. How could I go to England?

We had no money. There were no credit cards in Rhodesia in 1976.

What I *did* have was a bad dose of bronchitis and asthma.

But, how could I *not* go and say goodbye to my mother?

As I lay in bed, I tried to pray. I needed to hear from God—the same God I had wilfully turned away from ten years earlier. I crawled to my knees at the side of my bed, head in hands and found I could not pray—the words seemed to freeze at my head level. For ten years, I had refused to pray, and now I found I could not connect with God; my prayers did not even reach the ceiling. This added to the heartbreak. I felt so alone.

Brian was the praying member of the family! Throughout my years of rebellion, he'd continued to go to church, usually evensong, read his Bible, and prayed. He prayed for my mum that night, for me, for the decisions we needed to make. There was no way we could borrow any money; Brian's salary as a teacher was supplemented by my part-time work at the surgery. Our monthly expenses were covered, but there were very little savings.

I called Uncles Les and told him of the decision *not* to go due to finances. He told us Mum was in a coma and "peaceful".

My brothers were already on their way, Tony from Cape Town and Stuart from Bulawayo. They met up in London and travelled to Liverpool together but were too late to see her before she died on 17 July.

Her birthday card to me arrived the following day. I lay in bed and took the prescribed antibiotics. I felt stunned—my emotions frozen, bleak—and alone, despite being surrounded by my loving family.

### Turnaround

Again, I tried to pray, but again I found that block. By Sunday, I knew I needed to go to church. I headed for the nine fifteen service at Christchurch, leaving the children and Brian at home, arriving late so I could sneak into the back of the church without speaking to anyone. I can't remember the sermon or anything other than weeping throughout the entire service and feeling too unworthy to receive Communion. I do know that I said the confession—repenting from my heart. And I also know that confession was the release to allow my prayers to "get through".

Craig and Ann were confused and lost as I gave in to depression. They knew Grandma had gone, but their mother was not there for them either. One day, I heard a scuffle outside the toilet door as I sat there weeping and wallowing.

"What's she doing now?" Ann whispered.

Craig's voice replied, with a note of resignation, "Crying ... again!"

They were watching me through the keyhole! Grief and mourning were here to stay but, my children needed their mother, and I tried to pull myself together after that. My grief was fuelled by the feeling of guilt for not being there when she died.

During that time of mourning, I prayed a lot, almost constantly. Mum and I had spoken on the phone every day when she was alive. Living alone in Penhalonga, close to where Frelimo were ruling by the gun and training guerrillas for the Rhodesian war, she was at risk. I called daily to check that she was okay and encourage her, but those conversations, sharing my day with her, were vital for me too. Now I spoke with God instead of my mother. I called out to Him. How could I go on without her? Who would love me as my mum had loved me?

Then I heard His voice, for the first time ever. *I have given you a daughter—you will have that same relationship with her.*

## Things We Hold Dear

Tony and Stuart returned from England. They broke their journey in Salisbury (Harare) and delivered our mother's holiday suitcase to me—her clothes, her jewellery, her diary—bringing a part of her so close but confirming that she was not coming home. Stuart drove down to Bulawayo in Mum's car; Tony flew on to Cape Town.

Then there was the house to sort out. "Emoclew" standing empty, four kilometres from the Mozambique border with the liberation war still raging. Brian hired a truck, and we left the children with friends for the weekend, making the three-hour journey to Penhalonga . Mum's neighbours Les and Nola kindly gave us a bed for the two nights. I shared more tears with them and another neighbour, Sarah, Mum's new friends and Marg and Fred, brother Tony's in-laws.

Going into her home was hard. The view she loved was still there, the mountains filling the lounge windows with a glorious ever-changing vista. Her personality was everywhere, slippers just where she had stepped out of them the day she drove to our house. Clothing in the wardrobe still had her smell. Her Scripture Union daily readings with her notations in the margins, and there was the diary she'd kept during Dad's illness. Hardest was the document file, with detailed directions for me, where things were and what to do with them, confirming she knew her time on this earth was ending, and she intended to die in England. Her comment whenever things went wrong for her was usually, "My poor daughter!" Did I whinge and complain? She was always a blessing and never a weight.

On Saturday morning we visited her bank in Mutare, executors of her will, and arranged to rent the cottage, with basic furniture, to Anglo American.

Then came the task of packing the remainder and loading it all onto the truck. We drove away from Emoclew with heavy hearts, knowing we would never travel down that road again.

The terms of the will stated I would inherit all her personal goods; Mum knew I would distribute them. The linen and personal effects and some of her precious items were shared between the three of us. Stuart had recently divorced and was making a new home. So, on his next trip to Salisbury, he was able to take some items with fond memories for him. Her paintings of the sea were for Tony, and I had her glassware.

When I opened her jewellery box, there were notes relating to the more valuable pieces—turquoise ring for Lee (her birthstone) and gold earrings for Ann, wedding ring and engagement ring for me. There were lots of earrings, so I was able to choose some for Joss and for Fay and Gail. Mum had told Ann which precious item was for which precious person when she had helped Grandma sort out the jewel box. The peridot earrings that Mum had labelled for Stuart's wife were not delivered, as, by then, she was not Stuart's wife. When Stuart remarried, I gave them to my new sister-in-law, Wendy, who wore them on her wedding day. Peridot just happened to be one of her favourite stones!

## Family Comfort

That first Christmas was going to be hard. Mum and Dad had usually spent Christmas with us and were a big part of Craig and Ann's lives. There had been combined Christmases with Tony, Joss, and family too. On 16 December (the Day of the Covenant), Tony called from Cape Town gloating over the wonderful weather and breakfast on Boulders Beach.

"Why don't you come down for Christmas?" he said.

Just a throwaway line maybe, but it set us thinking. As usual, cost was the main problem, but Tony had a friend with a caravan we could borrow and put in their garden to house us all. So, we loaded our tiny Renault R4 up to the ceiling, mostly Mum's stuff, earmarked for Tony and Joss, and headed south.

The 2,000-mile journey was broken by a stopover in

Johannesburg. The second leg was taken in one shot, arriving at Zeekovlei just before midnight after eighteen hours driving.

We had intended sleeping in the car to avoid waking the family, but when we saw the house lights still on. "Surprise! We are here!"

Mugs of cocoa, hugs, and laughter ensued.

That family time was healing—not only for Tony and me but for all six grandchildren. Life had changed for them too, no grandparents phoning, writing, visiting, or sending gifts. But knowing they had loving family just a mile or 2,000 down the road, reassured them that there would be more good times together!

# FOURTEEN

# A Time to Be Born Again— with New Visions

Tragically, it had taken my mother's death to turn my face back towards God. My deepest regret is not turning back earlier; she would have been in her element going to church with her family. As a family, we started attending morning service at Christchurch, not every Sunday, but the turnaround had taken place.

## Salvation

In 1979, our church announced it would host a Lay Witness Mission weekend run by Africa Enterprise. This was something totally new to me, but I felt an overwhelming urge to be there. The dates coincided with Brian's final call-up, so it would mean going alone. But Craig and Ann were, at thirteen and fifteen, old enough to be left at home alone. I committed to a whole weekend at Church.

The weekend started on Friday night with a shared meal,

followed by a layman sharing his faith journey and testimony, receiving our questions, and responding with biblical teaching. On Saturday, a succession of speakers shared teaching and testimonies. The small group discussions were challenging, impacting, and thought-provoking.

The weekend culminated in a Sunday morning service with an altar call.

Christchurch's main two congregations were combined for one service, resulting in the church being jam-packed to overflowing. I was squashed in the middle of a crowded pew when the altar call came. My hand was raised, but the congestion was too restricting to wriggle out of the pew and go forward. That was the reason I gave myself! However, I *did* pray the sinner's prayer and, on that Sunday morning, acknowledged Jesus as my Lord and Saviour and asked Him to take over my life. And from that time, things started happening.

## God's Assurance

I became a regular worshipper at Christchurch on Sunday mornings. The services were liturgical, and a prayer is often said remembering those who had died:

> We pray for those we know who have died
> in the peace of Christ, and for those whose
> faith is known to you alone, and ask that all
> who have died in the hope of the resurrection,
> may enjoy, and share in the victory of our
> Lord Jesus Christ and fulness of joy in the
> fellowship of all your saints.
> Response: God of love, hear our prayer.

Whenever we prayed this prayer, I would mentally name my mother and other loved ones who had died but never my father. His statement that he had "made his peace with God" had not registered with me as his way of saying that he had accepted Jesus as his Lord and Saviour.

And then I became aware of sermons preached on the parable of the hired laborers. I heard them at church and on the radio; in my prayer time, my Bible fell open, and I read, from my NIV version of Matthew 20:1–6, the parable of the equally paid workers. I realised God was speaking to me from His word, and I prayed for revelation. He showed me that my father *had* turned to Him and was accepted into God's kingdom—albeit at the eleventh hour. But Dad was accepted according to Jesus's promise.

But wait—there's more! Another God-incidence was when I discovered that Peter W had left Zimbabwe and was now living in New Zealand. I tracked him down through the Wesleyan Methodist office and sent an email thanking him for spending time with my father in his dying days.

I told Peter I was not sure what Dad meant when he told me he had "made his peace with God". Peter W confirmed that he had led Dad to the Lord and that, "Les had, indeed, received Jesus as his Lord and Saviour!"

I look forward to meeting my dad again in glory!

## New Hope: Rhodesia becomes Zimbabwe

Back to Brian's "no timeframe dream on the back-burner". Eventually, the new shopping complex was completed, and the agent offered us one of the shops. It was small but in a good position, close to the Mall entrance and next to the building society, which would have steady foot traffic. We signed the papers and paid three months' rent in advance. My resignation was submitted, and I left the surgery after almost ten years.

Like expectant parents, we prepared for Fife Avenue Hardware to be born! Brian bought shelving at auction, which was painted and assembled with the help of our friends the Hammies. He also crafted the counter and exterior facade. The suppliers became friends, advising on fast moving stock and extending credit terms to cover the first months until we were established.

Our planning for Fife Avenue Hardware was against the backdrop of a much bigger picture. A new era was dawning in Rhodesia in 1980—one that gave us hope for the future. The Chimurenga War was over—no more call-ups for Brian. Rhodesian Front and United African National Council formed a coalition government. The first democratic election was scheduled for 27 to 29 February, with the expectation that Bishop Abel Muzorewa would be the next prime minister.

On 29 February, we watched in shock and alarm as the votes were tallied and the results revealed that the bishop had been soundly defeated! Our country would be led by the ZANU-PF leader, former terrorist Robert Mugabe.

Brian walked up and down most of that night, mentally exploring ways to reverse all we had committed to. Every penny we owned had been invested into our new venture, the lease signed for 3 years. I had resigned from my secure job. And now this uncertainty. Would white-owned businesses be nationalised? Would we be driven from the country? The following day, the majority of the people celebrated in true African style, with singing, ululating, and dancing in the streets.

That night, we shared dinner with the Hammies. The children played a board game, oblivious to life-changing events unfolding. Where would we go if we had to leave Rhodesia?

South Africa was the obvious place for Dee and Hugh, where they had relatives; England for us—the cold wet country of our birth? Or should we all learn Spanish and go to South America?

We tuned in to Robert Mugabe's post-election address to the nation on RTV. This was the first time I had heard him speak, and I was surprised and encouraged by the words coming from the lips of this seemingly educated man. No Pamberis! No clenched fists. No threats. He spoke of rebuilding a country prosperous for all, without racial discrimination, and wanting to join the Commonwealth. He presented as a moderate man.

Perhaps there was hope after all. Instead of learning Spanish and emigrating to South America, we all decided to emigrate to Zimbabwe!

The truth was, there was no way to cancel our shop lease without incurring a huge debt, so we decided to make the next three years count. Opening day was scheduled for Monday 11 March 1980, Brian's forty-fourth birthday!

## Shop Owners: A Dream Realised

There was an air of excitement as the shops opened one by one—a pharmacy, a building society, and six boutique stores lined the arcade leading to the supermarket, offering a variety of retail therapy. The owner/operators of the small shops became colleagues and work mates, sharing knowledge and a camaraderie as we each transformed soulless empty spaces into inviting individual realms.

Sally's gift shop was the realisation of her dream, motivating her to abandon a career in radiography. We already had a connection through the surgery and became friends over our shared experience as rookie shop owners. Roger, well known antiques expert, assisted by Bennie, raised the tone of the arcade, offering treasures from days gone by in his Aladdin's cave. Brian designed and made rotating display units for the unique handmade silver jewellery created by Debbie in the shop next door. Paddy, a lively TV personality, supported his wife Joy in her venture of owning a ladies' clothing boutique. (Was the Xmas knicker tree his idea?!)

## Growing Clientele

The supermarket at the far end of the arcade provided a steady stream of potential customers just waiting to be lured inside the small shops. Relationships were formed as residents from local apartment blocks popped in to browse or say hi, en-route to buying tonight's dinner. Frank, one of the patients at the surgery, regularly brought me a doughnut when he bought his own morning tea. Faith discussions would happen spontaneously, possibly because my own faith was growing after many years of stagnation. Mike would stop by to chat. He was a fun caring Catholic solo dad, struggling to bring up his boys in the fear of God. Fran, an SDA member, shared her beliefs and her knowledge of nutrition and "correct" vegetarian eating—inviting me to events.

Two other very different customers stick in my memory. One morning, when I was alone in the shop, a very dishevelled man with a wild look in his eyes and an angry scowl on his face strode through the open door. Without a word to me, he opened the backing to the window and started removing tools from the display. I froze on the spot—a thief!! There was no weapon visible, but he displayed a fierce intentionality. The pile of tools assembled on the floor was growing. I knew I had to stop him. This was my stock, probably not even paid for yet!

A quick prayer: "Protect me please, Lord!" And I caught the man's hand. "Can I help you?"

The man grunted, snatched his hand away from me, and gathered up the pile of tools in his arms. Instead of walking out of the door, he crossed the shop and dumped them onto the counter. Rummaging in his pocket, he pulled a wad of crumpled notes and thrust them in my face. In that moment, I recognised he was a former insurgent, now labelled a war veteran. Each combatant had received a lump sum from the government, and this man was using his pay-out to buy tools to start a new life!

His English was very limited, but he managed to communicate his needs. I showed him a selection of tools from the shelves and then tallied up the cost of those he selected. He left, still unsmiling but with his money well spent and my good wishes for his new venture! I sank onto my stool, shaking— deep breaths. "Thank You, Lord!" That was the largest sale I had ever clocked up.

The other customer is remembered for very different reasons. The evening was cold, dark, and wet. I was closing the shop, later than usual, when a lady entered wearing a damp fur coat. She was holding an African violet in each hand, having collected them from the display trolley at the door. Her face looked vaguely familiar, but no name sprang to mind—maybe because she looked very tired as she sat down heavily on the chair beside the counter.

"Are these hard to look after?" she asked. "I want to give them as thank you gifts but not if they're going to die quickly."

I assured her that they would flower for many weeks. "The trick is finding the right place, dappled light without direct sun and water into the tray at the bottom."

We chatted about the heavy rain while I packaged the plants. "Can you manage them both?" I asked.

"The car is just outside," she said.

I handed her the box of plants.

"Goodnight and thank you for your help," she said with a lovely smile.

When I saw the chauffeur come to the door and relieve her of the plants, I realised I had been talking with Sally Mugabe—Zimbabwe's beautiful first First Lady.

# FIFTEEN

# A Time to Tear—and to Mend

## Health wobble

The shop was fast taking on my personality instead of Brian's! Dormant artistic flare surfaced as I hand-painted asbestos containers in eye-catching designs; new skills were developed as I learned window display, grouping African violets and other flowering plants together to present garden appeal. Large pots and wrought-iron stands soon overflowed onto the exterior— eye appeal became the buzz word. The indoor space housed a variety of hardware items, not quite "tacks to anchors" but almost; we had everything from nails, nuts, and bolts to hand tools and even bicycles. And we stocked paint in all sizes from tiny pots to ten-litre tins.

It was those large ten-litre paint tins that revealed a health wobble. I had accredited severe pain in my back to moving those heavy tins around without help. Dr Joe sent me for an X-ray. The results were not what we expected—no bone or muscle damage, just a huge ugly gallstone!

He came into the shop pretending to sharpen his scalpel, assuming I would want to have this removed ASAP. But I considered taking another route. The stone was too large to cause a tube blockage, but it had lodged in the corner of the gall bladder and was pressing on other organs and causing inflammation. This was the medical analysis when looking at this rock on the X-ray.

So, I made some decisions. Firstly, I would tackle it with prayer. Brian and I asked the Lord to heal the inflammation and take away the pain. I adjusted my diet, reducing fat intake and monitoring cream and wine! A strong young man, George, was hired to help with the lifting, as he learned cycle repairs and picture framing. I agreed to keep in touch with Dr Joe and not ignore symptoms if they recurred.

This was my first foray into prayer for healing. I believe God has been directing me in this previously ignored area of my faith. And of course, I could not learn about healing prayer without something to heal!

Inflammation has flared up intermittently, usually triggered by something out of the ordinary, such as a time of extreme grief. There have been no tests or X-rays to confirm if the stone is still there or has been prayed away. Any discomfort in that area is treated by prayer.

## Another Career Change for Brian?

The original plan for the shop was that Brian would continue teaching until the shop was making enough money for me to step back into a support role. Brian would then start his home maintenance business. As the sales increased and the revenue grew, retired engineer Ken was employed for one day a week to give me a free day and time to do the books. The figures showed we were getting closer to our goal. Brian was planning and working towards starting his maintenance business—until he met Hugh at a men's prayer breakfast!

The agricultural college where Hugh was principal had a vacancy for a lecturer in Building and Land Conservation. Brian's qualifications ticked all the boxes, and he was enticed by the prospect of moving back to country living. But this would radically reverse our plans. The shop we had birthed would need to be sold. We would be walking away from that dream. It would also mean a huge upheaval for the family, leaving our home and putting Ann into another school as a weekly boarder for her final two senior years.

Craig voiced his favour of the move, but as he was heading to Pietermaritzburg University, his vote did not count! I was definitely against. My response was, "No way! Out of the question. Count me out." We had given up so much to get this shop up and running. I was just beginning to see it as a success, to relax a little. And now Brian was suggesting we sell!

Hugh invited us to Sunday lunch, and we drove out of town after church. Dulcie welcomed us to their home, and the afternoon was spent chatting to their family, exploring the campus and the farm, and meeting several other staff members. Hugh showed us the house that would become our home if we said yes. It was identical to my parents' home in Chinhoyi. I already knew the layout of the rooms. But the view beyond the garden was wider with vistas of open bush beyond the tennis courts. Carrots were being dangled!

Back home, we discussed our options. I had no desire to change our lives but recognised Brian's attraction to country life. My suggestion was that, if Brian really wanted this job, he should either travel the twenty-five miles each way daily or weekly board out there.

Craig's response shook me. "So, Mum, are you going to break up this family for a shop?"

I knew I needed to pray about this, very seriously! It would be a great career opportunity for Brian but a tremendous wrench for me. In addition to selling the shop, it would mean leaving friends, church, our home. And I was concerned about Ann, in her O level year. How would she cope with moving to another school, weekly boarding, and leaving behind all her school friends? This was not what I wanted for her. The head teacher was consulted and reassured me she believed Ann was secure enough to make the adjustment. A place was found at Girls High, a boarding school in the city.

## Falling into place

We had no idea how or where to sell a shop as a going concern. More prayer! Before we had even started to investigate, a man came into the shop, looked around, and began chatting with Brian. He'd recently started a maintenance and repair service from his home but wanted to combine this with a hardware shop, run by his wife! He introduced himself as Gary, asking Brian's guidance on how to start out.

When Brian told him we were planning to sell, the discussions became more focussed. Was this a coincidence or a God-incidence? They were a family similar to ours. They had two teenaged children and belonged to their local church in Chisipite. Negotiations started almost spontaneously; the shop's balance sheet was examined, and record of the most recent stock count produced. We arrived at an agreed selling price. The deed was done.

Now we just needed tenants for our Greystone Park home. This did not take long! There were many applicants on open home day. A newly married couple applied and seemed the perfect choice. They were happy to employ Gabriel and

Loveness and allow their family to continue living in the staff cottage.

Moving was a surprisingly grieving experience—emotionally draining. My tears flowed incessantly. I told myself it was just bricks and mortar, but I grieved for the memories and experiences enclosed within those walls—walls I had scrubbed, painted, papered, and enhanced with pictures. And there was the garden, created from scratch.

Brian assured me it was just a season. We would be back one day. But I felt that this was an ending, and in many ways, it was. We did eventually return to our home, but I returned a different person

We said our goodbyes to Loveness and Gabriel and headed along the Lomagundi Road, towards a new season of our lives.

# SIXTEEN

# A Time to Plant

## New Vision

And a new season it was—a God-focussed season! The freedom from daily work commitments allowed me to consolidate my renewed faith and work out my walk with Jesus. I can now see this transplanting was God's plan. There was time to curl up in front of the fire as the weather cooled, reading my Bible and books by inspirational authors. Dulcie introduced me to the local Tape Library, which hired out inspirational messages by Christian leaders. Vacuuming was done to loud, uplifting worship songs, and David Pawson or Derek Prince kept me company when ironing or cooking.

Dulcie also introduced me to the Esthers, a group of women who had prayed for our country and its people throughout the war years and were still on their knees, joined by the occasional Mordecai! Their monthly meetings were a platform for shared testimonies and local inspirational speakers. Brian and I joined Bible study groups on campus and the local branch of International Christian Embassy Jerusalem, ICEJ, where our eyes were opened to the Jewish roots of our Christian faith.

With Craig at Uni in South Africa and Ann weekly boarding at school in town, a new weekly pattern took shape. On Monday morning, I would drive the twenty-five miles into the city, deliver Ann to school, and then attend 8 a.m. communion at the cathedral, with coffee and catch-up afterwards. Friday was another town day, collecting Ann for the weekend. The days in between were my own; I had freedom to attend midweek meetings, listen to tapes, and deepen my faith.

The profit from selling the shop had been invested for Craig and Ann's university fees; cost of living in the rural area was lower than in town, so additional income from me wasn't needed. We made friends with staff members; enjoyed tennis on Saturdays; and attended our new Church, St Paul's. I relaxed into this new lifestyle, which Brian had assured me would go on forever. "You will never need to work again!"

And then things changed.

## Lost Investment

In 1991, Zimbabwe's Economic Structural Adjustment Program (ESAP) was introduced. By the following year, the stock market was affected, causing financial insecurity! Shares we had bought for 110cents, anticipating increase, dropped rapidly in value down to 7cents! Sales on the local stock market increased as people strove to realise a portion of their investment. Our decision was to hold onto them in the hope that, one day, there would be recovery.

We scraped up enough money to pay for Craig's last semester at university, but Brian was now making "back to work" noises! He suggested I register with an employment agency. I dragged my heels during the September school holidays when Ann was home. During the first week of term, we received an invoice from Pietermaritzburg University, fees for the following year due by the end of December. Brian suggested I combine collecting Ann from school on Friday with registering with an employment agency. Here we go! My days of freedom, "never having to work again", were about to disappear in a puff of smoke. But I knew there was no other way to raise the money.

Those months at home had been a vital time of learning to put my walk with my Lord first, redirecting my thoughts and aspirations. Getting back into a daily work routine would be hard. But even harder would be driving twenty-five miles each way!

## Compliant wife

On Friday morning, I completed registration forms at the employment agency, handed them to the receptionist with my CV, and was heading for the door when I heard, "That's interesting." She was reading my CV and checking it against another form. "Please wait a moment," she said and disappeared into an inner office.

What had I done wrong? Was my CV not updated in correct current format? A moment later she ushered me into the inner office and introduced me to her manager, Pamela.

"I received a request this morning" she said, "For a credit controller with a company very close to where you live. Your application form lists a lot of accounting experience. Any credit control?"

"Not really," I confessed, "but at the surgery and the shop, there was the occasional bounced cheque or non-payment to chase up."

123

I had never held the title of credit controller or managed a debtor's section larger than me.

"Hmmm," said Pamela. "It won't be easy finding someone willing to work out of town for this company, but it's just a few minutes from where you live. Let me give them a call."

I returned to the waiting room while she spoke on the telephone, expecting to be told, "No, sorry. They want someone with experience."

Pamela's head peeped around the door. "Can you call in this afternoon," she asked, "before four o'clock?"

This was *not* the reply I'd anticipated! But I agreed to call in on the way home. It would probably be a wasted journey. I could never claim to be a credit controller! But I could leave my CV with the company against future vacancies, and Brian would see that I was trying.

The company covered a large acreage, with warehouse-sized buildings for blending wines. There was also a residential village for staff. We had driven past this huge complex, literally five-minute's drive from the college, on every trip into town, without giving more than a glance.

Shortly after three o'clock, I was shown into an office and introduced to the personnel manager, Ken, and the company secretary, Hugh. Ken pleasantly questioned me about previous work and then suggested I give the job a go, on three months' probation, at an attractive salary. And could I start on Monday?

Brian's reaction to my news can only be described as gobsmacked. He was astounded it had all come together so quickly and delighted we would be able to meet the uni deadline, although he still felt guilty to be going back on his promise to me that I'd never have to work again.

It was confirmation from Proverbs 3:5–6 (NLT): "Trust in the LORD with all your heart, do not depend on your own understanding. Seek his will in all you do, and he will show you which path to take."

I *had* been seeking His will during my sabbatical! Both Brian and I had been praying for our way forward faith wise, and latterly praying desperately about how to pay the university fees. No doubt, this was a God thing! He had given me eight months at home to study and grow in faith, almost a gestation time. He had heard our prayers and my grumps about the twenty-five-mile trip either way and blessed me with a job I was not qualified for!

## My Turn for a New Career

At 8 a.m. sharp on Monday morning, I walked through the reception doors and was shown into Ken's office to await the arrival of the staff bus. The debtors' team was a pleasant group of six ladies, welcoming and supportive as I floundered my way around unfamiliar methods of accounting. The company had scheduled the installation of a computerised system for the following year. But meanwhile, data was compiled and delivered daily to a company in town, who provided weekly updated printouts. I had never used computerised accounting; my experience had been with ledgers, not computer printouts. There were so many processes to learn, so many credit controllers of large stores and small shop owners to interact with telephonically or meet face to face, so many customers' issues to resolve and goals to achieve—weekly and monthly!

This was all new and challenging. With much to learn and many targets to meet, I felt inadequate and began to lose sleep, dreading going to work in the morning. As the first month was completed, we were praying for wisdom, and direction. I did not want to be a credit controller, and Brian was sad that I needed to go back to work at all! My first salary was deposited in the university account—halfway there. I decided to complete the three-month probation and pay next year's fees but not accept the permanent position. Then I would look for something more to my liking, focussed on people, not figures.

Ken called me into his office a week later, just five weeks into my probation time. My heart sank! Did this mean my work did not measure up to the company's expectations and I would be told to go? Would I be unable to compete the probation and earn the much-needed dollars?

Anxiously, I climbed the stairs and entered Ken's office. Three of the top brass, drinking their morning coffee, smiled a welcome. Hugh again, plus company accountant Des. Ken announced they had been reviewing the month-end figures, which were "excellent". They believed I was the right person for the job, and they had drawn up a contract ignoring the rest of the probation time and increased my salary.

I took the contract home to study. Apart from the salary increase, there were bonuses, discounts, and use of the company holiday cottage! This was the first job I'd ever had with "perks". Plus, another carrot—of training in computerised accounting when the new system was installed the following year—was dangled. Management did not see my performance as poor and was pleased with the results. This truly was a godsend! How could I refuse?

I signed on the dotted line and only signed off twenty years later!

Camping trip to Vumba

Our Wedding

Fay and Gail

Announcing Baby on the way

# AUTUMN

# SEVENTEEN

# A Time to Accept New Experiences

## God's agenda?

Our prayers had not been answered in the way we expected or wanted. Had God directed me to this workplace? Was this part of His plan? Over the years, I grew to believe it was. God's plan is always to draw people closer to Him and bring them into His kingdom. When I signed the contract, I had no idea of God's wider agenda.

The first inkling was when Cheryl joined me one morning at tea break. "I hear that the college has Bible study groups." She said, "Could I join one of those? And my friend Mandy?"

Operational staff were housed on site, and Cheryl was the wife of the winery manager. She lived next door to Mandy, Ken's wife. Both women had recently become Christians and were thirsty for more. I expressed my doubts about a college Bible study. "The groups are in the evening. And they're mostly students, not many members of staff." It wasn't the ideal support group to spiritually feed the faith of two young mums.

But then I had a thought. "We could start a group here if

you like. After work? I could be at your house just after four. Would that suit you and Mandy?"

We agreed to give it a try—keep to an hour to avoid interfering with family mealtime. A farming friend, Diana, joined Cheryl and Mandy. They would get together in the afternoon for coffee and catch up, waiting for me to finish work and join them at four. Together, we worked through Scripture Union material, each exploring our faith and focussing on deepening our relationship with God through Jesus our Saviour—a tentative step on our faith journeys.

Our time together included prayer for our families; all three women had non-believing husbands, so we were able to pray together for their salvation. God worked in Ken and Phil's lives, in different ways, and they each came to faith in Jesus Christ. The ladies moved on to deeper Bible studies. But the way was opened to me for times of prayer at lunchtime with the men over issues the company was facing.

## Different Strokes

The following year, the much-anticipated computer system was installed. New techniques were learned by the team, and Roland joined the company as the computer operator. The system was one of those huge cabinets, with figure of eight tapes spinning around sorting and storing data. Roland backed up all input twice daily, printed reports and monthly statements, and learned to deal with random power cuts and system crashes. I was his designated assistant for the month-end run, compiling the month's data with operating figures and printing statements. Between the times of frantic activity, there were lengthy periods when nothing much happened. We could chat while the machine churned. These were times of sharing our beliefs and what God was doing in our lives. Roland shared his Jehovah's Witness faith, my first encounter with this belief. We had deep discussions about scriptures and their meanings and applications and the occasional disagreement.

One Saturday, I was preparing material for a Bible study, and the scripture I wanted eluded me, so I asked Roland for help.

"Hey, Roland, you know your Bible well! Where does it say no one can say Jesus is Lord except by the power of the Holy Spirit?"

"There is no such scripture," he answered.

"What! Of course there is."

Now I had to find it. So I borrowed the Bible Roland always kept in his desk drawer. "Here it is.":

> Therefore, I would have you know that no one when speaking by God's spirit says, "Jesus be accursed," and nobody can say, "Jesus is Lord," except by holy spirit. (1 Corinthians 12:3, NWT, published by *Watchtower*)

The wording was almost the same, but no capitals for Holy Spirit. That's when I discovered Jehovah Witnesses did not believe in a triune God; they do not know the Holy Spirit as a person but just as our own spirits becoming holy. We had some really deep discussion that day.

## Surprise Healing

Since our move to Gwebi, we had been attending morning service at St Paul's Anglican Church. Ann came with us but found the liturgy and the older congregation hard going; she preferred more charismatic worship. So, occasionally Ann and I would make the twenty-five-mile journey into town to attend Sunday evening worship at a more charismatic church.

One such night, we arrived at Rhema Church not knowing the church had been holding a revival conference for the past three days, with speakers from all over the world, and this Sunday night service was the climax. They were almost swinging from the chandeliers! The praise, as always, was uplifting—great musicians, rousing hymns and choruses, gifted support singers.

The tempo started to soften into more worshipful songs after a while, and I prepared to hear the message. But a prophecy was given, which set everyone alight again, and the joyful praise resumed—louder and livelier than before! There was dancing in the aisles, some falling on the ground. My thought was that this was OTT—more exhibitionism than worshipping Jesus, the King of Kings and Lord of Lords. I sat down and quietly prayed, setting myself apart from the rest of the congregation.

That's when I heard the command. "All those whose backs are out of alignment, be *healed* in Jesus's name."

I looked up from my quiet prayers and saw one of the speakers, Casey Treat, in the centre of the stage, arms raised and outstretched.

My back was out of alignment. A lumbar vertebra had been broken in an accident when I was fourteen and had healed unaided but irregularly, causing me great pain and some restriction of movement due to touching the sciatic nerve. There had been a variety of treatments over the years, but the pain returned and sometimes my left leg seized.

As I heard that command, I also felt hands on my lower back. Someone behind me was putting hands through the gap in the lower part of the chair to lay hands on my back. Was that someone who knew me and knew about my back? Or had they received a word from God? I turned to see who that was and saw that the entire row of seats was empty! Not a single person was close enough to touch me. And what's more, the chair I was sitting on was solid—no gap in the back.

I felt humbled, rebuked by God for judging the worship to be too loud. It was as though He rapped me on the knuckles and said, "My people can praise and worship me however they wish—straight from their hearts not their heads!"

God may have rebuked me, but He also healed me. There was no feeling of heat in my back or bones moving back into place as commanded—nothing at all. *But* I have never again had that crippling sciatic pain I had lived with for forty years! God healed me and used the healing to teach me that *He is Lord*, and we are born to worship Him, and different people worship Him in different ways.

## The Lord's Protection

During my years with the company, Zimbabwe went through almost continuous political upheaval. These were times when we needed to trust that God really was in charge. One day, young Christine, a member of my team, was relieving on reception. She called me, whispering into the phone, "Mrs Bishop, can you hear me?" She was obviously frightened. "There are men here with guns! They want to see you—about a stopped order."

Oh, no! A quick prayer, "Help, Lord."

I grabbed the file on my desk, called the security officer, John, in his office at the far end of the winery, and told him I was heading for reception to rescue Christine.

She was cowering behind her desk when I arrived. Sure

enough, there were two men in camouflage, with AK rifles slung over their shoulders. The third man, smartly dressed in a suit, was recognisable as a government minister.

Keeping a calm and smiling countenance, I extended my hand to the former freedom fighter, now cabinet minister. "Mr T, a pleasure to meet you. How may I help?"

"Why have you stopped the order being delivered to my liquor store?" he demanded, naming the outlet.

"The manager had no cash to pay for the order," I replied, explaining, "The invoice clearly states, 'Notes only.'"

"My manager had a cheque to pay. Why would your driver refuse the cheque from my manager?"

I took a deep breath. "This store is rated notes only, sir. Payment in hard cash on delivery is required now because previous cheques have not been honoured. The driver could not leave the order without payment."

He looked genuinely surprised. "Why would cheques bounce?" he demanded. "The store is making plenty of money."

"You will need to discuss that with your bank, Mr T. We have a company policy, which applies to everyone, no favourites. If three cheques are dishonoured, the rating becomes notes. If no cash is available, the order is uplifted and redelivered at an agreed time."

I removed the three bounced cheques from the file and handed them to him. "The signatory on the cheque is the name we have registered as the owner of this store. Is that correct?" I asked. "He has been advised of the change to notes only."

"Aaaaaaah," he said. "That is my nephew. He runs my store. I own it."

It transpired that his nephew was pocketing the cash from sales instead of banking it—hence, the bounced cheques.

"Going forward, Mr T. If you can assure me there will

be cash available to pay for this order, I will arrange a special delivery this afternoon."

He agreed, we shook hands again, and the trio left—just as the security officer and his support group burst through the door. Christine and I headed for the tea room to stop the shaking.

But the situation had been resolved without a shot being fired.

# EIGHTEEN

# A Time for Gathering

## More Change

Zimbabwe as a nation was experiencing more uncertain times—dissension between the political parties and rumours of atrocities by the Fifth Brigade. The identity of the country's premier agricultural college began to change. Hugh retired, and the new principal arrived, ready and eager for transformation. The staff became unsettled, and some looked for other posts.

Was it time for us to leave too? What were our options? We discussed buying a small farm, worked out how much our Greystone Park home would sell for and submitted a bid on a farm for sale in Marondera. The owner took us on a guided tour, and our minds went into overdrive as we visualised a new life on the farm. That night, Craig worked until the early hours on a farm plan. Brian and I prayed for "God to be in control"—really meaning that our offer would be accepted!

We were all deeply disappointed when we were outbid. But in the light of future events, we would come to see this as God's protection and direction.

As the horrors of the Gukurahundi genocide began to

surface, we assessed our future and decided to move back into town. Brian resigned from government education after twenty-five years of service, with a plan to start his own company already percolating. We left the college on a wet December day, without ceremony, returning to our Greystone Park home.

The move was timely for our children too. Ann was back in Harare from her Hotel Management training in Bulawayo, on a term's placement at a city hotel, and Craig had secured a holiday job on a Mtepatepa farm for the University holidays

## Change in the Church

On Sunday, we headed for morning service, eager to be back in our "old church" with familiar faces. But we discovered the congregation was experiencing an interregnum, a season without a priest in charge. Visiting priests kept the services going but attendance had dropped, and families had drifted away. The remaining congregation was praying intently for new leadership.

Interregnums are times of uncertainty but can also provide opportunity for regrouping, refocus, and growth, when the faithful get out of the pews and use the gifts God has given them. With that wonderful gift of hindsight, I can see that is exactly what happened to me, when I was drawn into new ministries without consciously recognising God's guidance.

John and Jean W, recently retired from their church in England, arrived in Borrowdale two weeks before Christmas. John was a reserved, gentle Anglican priest—nothing flashy but with a solid practical faith in Jesus. Initially, the cathedral had offered them a position, but he and Jean accepted the opportunity to be interim pastors in Borrowdale, until the arrival of the new priest and his family from the Lowveld.

When chatting to John and Jean after the Christmas Eve crib service, I discovered they were celebrating Christmas alone. We were on our own for Christmas Day too, as Craig and Ann were both working. I had planned a lowkey meal of roast chicken for the two of us, not exactly welcoming festive fare for our new priest!

Then I remembered a large leg of lamb in the freezer so invited John and Jean for lunch next day and went home to defrost it. Early on Christmas morning, I started prepping the meat, only to discover a very high smell! This was a leg of karakul lamb, lots of fat, which could have been the reason for the smell; the flesh was not discoloured. So, I cut off all the fat; soaked the leg in a solution of vinegar, pushed rosemary under the skin, wrapped it in foil—and prayed the promise of Jesus over it: "Lord, your word in Mark 16 tells us who believe that we will drink poison and not be harmed! Surely this applies to eating dodgy lamb!"

Brian was a little anxious, but the shops were all closed; no alternative food was available. I prayed the meat would not harm anyone and would taste good! The meat was put in the oven while we went to church; it looked and smelled good when we returned. I confess to being slightly anxious, checking for taste and smell, maybe lacking faith. So I cooked the chicken too, providing a choice.

John said grace and asked that the Lord would *bless* the food to our bodies. And the Lord did, as no one had any ill effects. Imagine if I had killed off the new priest before he had time to regather the flock! Months later, when I knew them well, I confessed to Jean and was delighted with her genuine laughter. She said, it was just the sort of thing she would have done.

## Home Group

John's plan to strengthen and pull the church together again was with small groups, and everyone was encouraged to join one of the groups. Brian and I found one close to our home, run by Henri and Margaret. The group met in the home of a widow with a young son. It was a new home group forming, so we did not feel like outsiders and soon were melded into a real family feel.

There were twelve people of mixed ages and stages—a widow, a divorcee, couples with children still at home, and one set of grandparents—a mixed bag! We shared uplifting and inspirational evenings of Bible study and also social events—lunches, picnics, friendships. Another single mum joined us several months later, bringing her wonderful gift of music. Dee had a lovely voice and was an accomplished guitarist, so we enjoyed singing praise songs in our home group. This prompted us to approach John W to share an idea for a non-liturgical evening service.

## Prayer and Praise

Our home group stood around after the nine fifteen service, cups in hand, waiting for a chance to talk to John W about our plan. John H got in there first. "Hey there, John," he said in his Liverpool accent. "Our home group has been singing some great choruses since Dee joined us. Is there any chance of us having a prayer and praise evening service instead of evensong?"

Everyone held their breath, eyes focused on our shy interim priest.

John W's face lit up. "That sounds exactly what Jean and

I have been talking about," he said. "Let me have a look at the schedule and see where we can allocate one Sunday evening a month as prayer and praise Sunday."

Evensong was reduced to two Sundays a month, interspersed with a healing service and prayer and praise—something for everyone. Music practice was on Saturday afternoon before the Sunday prayer and praise service, a time to learn new worship songs. Inspirational speakers were invited from other churches.

## Sunday School

One of the things that had gone to the wall during the interregnum was Sunday school. This had entirely fizzled out, and the children sat through services with bored expressions or leaning on parents, definitely not being fed at their own spiritual level. I asked John what was happening.

"I really don't know," he said. "Several families left when the last priest left. I'll see what can be done."

After another few weeks of restless children in church, I approached John again. "John, any news about Sunday school restarting?"

"Not yet," was his response.

"And I hear there is no youth group either," I said. "The teens need something to do on Friday nights."

Was I just stirring? Being a busybody? My own children were grown. John looked at me directly. "Usually, the person who is asking the questions is the one God is speaking to," he replied. "Martin has been asking the same questions, so have a word with him." He smiled as he walked away, leaving me feeling stunned.

What, me? Sunday school and youth group! I had not

been part of these ministries when my own children were in those age groups.

Perhaps I could start with Sunday school. I prayed about it, but there was no direct word from God. So, on Thursday morning. I headed for the parish office and handed the secretary, Sue, an ad to go into the pew leaflet she was preparing:

> Sunday school teachers needed for all age groups. Please prayerfully consider taking a class. No experience needed, just a love for the Lord and our children.
>
> Phone Marie, 884153, to chat.

Secretary Sue promised to give my phone number to any volunteers and handed me a box containing Scripture Union materials with the same weekly message for four age levels. I sorted out the lesson for the coming week. Now we need some songs and music! I was a bit out of touch with kiddies' songs. Do they still like "Father Abraham" and "Allelu, Allelu,Allelu Alleluia, Praise ye the Lord?

There were no phone calls, no volunteers. So, I realised I was going it alone this week. About fifteen children all sizes followed me out of church during the second hymn to the area I'd set up in the hall earlier. The two songs worked; the actions using surplus energy so that they were ready to sit and listen—when I had breath enough to teach.

We finished with a colouring in time so they each had something to show Mum and Dad and a reminder of what they had learned. Phew! I had survived.

*But* I welcomed the help offered by two mums after the service. They were both encouraging about the SU material, and Alison, a guitarist, would be happy to take care of the singing side. A team was growing. And it continued to grow, with previous Sunday school teachers who had been waiting to get the nod offering their services. Sunday school was up and running again!

## Youth Group with Martin

Martin sought me out at teatime on that first Sunday, telling me that his little girl, Nicky, had really enjoyed Sunday school. Also, John had pointed him towards me in respect to the Friday night youth group.

Oh, boy! I showed him the material at teen level, which had also come in the SU box, and Martin took some away to have a look and see where we went from there. We both agreed to pray about it.

During the next few weeks, the number of volunteer Sunday school teachers grew. And Jean, a regular at the 7.30 a.m. service, offered to take over management of the Sunday school roster, completely allowing me to step back. When she heard that Martin and I were planning to get the youth group going she was delighted! It was just what her twelve-year-old daughter wanted (or needed).

School holidays were starting at the end of the week, so Martin and I decided the new term would be the ideal time to begin. We used the holidays to work out a format and program for next term. The evenings would start with free time as the young gathered; cold drinks or hot chocolate and biscuits would be available. The hall was large enough for indoor ball games, skittles, or table tennis using the table stored in a back room. We planned group activities for the first hour—fish n chips suppers or pizzas, even a pancake making night! The second hour would move to teaching using the SU material, with occasional movies, dividing into smaller groups for discussion.

Visiting speakers were invited—youth leaders from other churches. One speaker encouraged the youth to share their favourite pop song and then speedily typed the words onto a screen and asked the person to read what he or she had been singing! There were some red faces that night.

A piece of advice given to me by Andy S has never been forgotten. I'd shared my concern about reaching the unchurched young folk who were coming with their friends; one was particularly disruptive. How could we reach him, draw him in, not turn him away with rules and restrictions? Andy reminded me that Jesus had said, "Feed my sheep" (John 21: 17, NIV). "Focus on Jesus' lambs," Andy said, "and others will follow."

## New Priest

As John and Jean's six months came to an end, they took their intended positions at the cathedral. There was excited anticipation as our new rector arrived with his family. The Lord had heard the prayers of His people for a young family to reach out to other young families in the parish. There had never been a family living in the rectory—only couples or single priests. Now, at long last, there would be children playing in the gardens, and those children would bring their friends home. The youth group would grow. And as an added blessing, the rector's entire family was *musical*! Company for Alison on her guitar. Little did we know how much company! Pauline was a music teacher, and any church child registered in her classes was given a place in the church youth orchestra and played at the nine fifteen service.

The nine fifteen was the most "praisey" service, using the 1975 liturgy and aimed at families, with lively hymns accompanied by the youth orchestra. There were two other morning services offering different types of worship, each attracting different folk. The day started at six thirty with a short communion service, no singing, no passing the peace. The seven thirty was a more traditional prayer book service with a choir, music on the organ, and breakfast in the hall afterward. The three congregations were like three separate churches, very little intermingling. Even the home groups were compiled of members from their Sunday service time slot.

James and Pauline planned events to bring all the groups together, teaching evenings, and shared meals. In their second year, the annual fundraiser for the orphanage in our parish was a game changer. It was not the usual cake/book sale. James planned a pantomime! Cinderella! And he suggested *everyone* be involved in some way—acting, singing and dancing, making and gathering costumes, applying stage make-up, preparing scenery, advertising, printing programmes, selling ticket, and working the front of the house on performance nights. There were months of fun nights— rehearsing, painting scenery, and sometimes just engaging in discussions.

Performances were in the local school hall—for three nights! James and Pauline's plan worked, and three very different congregation groups were blended together.

We became one large church family.

# NINETEEN

# A Time to Heal

## Wholeness

During John W's time as interim priest at Borrowdale, he encouraged all three congregations to attend midweek teachings. One of these, on healing and wholeness, revolutionised my understanding of healing!

John explained how we are three-part beings, drawing three overlapping circles—body, soul (our mind and emotions), and spirit. Each is affected by the other. Easiest to recognise is when the body is not fed well or sleep-deprived, we feel unwell. When the body is not at its best, we feel down, and our souls, our thoughts, and emotions are affected—body affecting soul. So where does the spirit come into all of this? The spirit is over both; we can ask the spirit to take control of both our body and our soul.

John said, in his very quiet manner that, when he feels unwell, he stands before the mirror, lays a hand on his own head, and claims the lordship of Jesus over his entire life. "I am fearfully and wonderfully made by Almighty God, my Heavenly Father. Jesus has redeemed me by His blood, and by His stripes I have already been healed. There is no room for you, Satan. I am a child of God through Jesus. So *get away from me*! Holy Spirit, fill me now in every corner of my being with Jesus's life-giving resurrection power so I can continue to do the things God intends me to do."

John shared that he then carries on with his day and suddenly realises that whatever was ailing him has gone! Surprise, surprise. It is in God's word, and it is *true*. It's just a matter of knowing God's word and speaking it out—not just thinking it or reading it but *speaking* it.

John W's teaching also highlighted the authority Jesus gave to His believers in Mark 17:18 (NIV): "They will place hands on sick people, and they will get well." I now accept Jesus's great commission, pray with authority, and don't ask God to do it all.

This was all entirely new to me. I resolved to follow John's method and take authority according to God's word. Over the years, this has become my way of dealing with illness. I declare that disease is not from God; it is from the other fella! I rebuke the illness, as Jesus did when healing Peter's mother-in-law in Luke 4:39 (NIV): "He bent over her and rebuked the fever and it left her." Tell the enemy he is a defeated foe, overthrown by the blood of Jesus, and he needs to go! I also address the affected part of my body and tell it, "Be healed. Be restored to the perfect way God made you."

## Health and Healing

Ironically, it was a health issue—and the way other Christians deal with health and healing—that was the bone of contention between Brian and me, almost shattering our marriage beyond repair. This was during the early years of our marriage, when we were longing for children—a time I have called *barrenness*.

Brian, in his own search for truth, had been drawn into Christian Science and looked at spiritual healing as the answer to our infertility problem, not medical or surgical treatments. My response was to reject both the method and source and turn away from God. Was God using His healing to build faith in Him? And had I missed that opportunity, resulting in years in the wilderness, my face turned from Him? God did heal the barrenness in my life, initially by sending children in need of care and then by blessing me with my own babies.

Since I'd given my life to Jesus, there had been a steady progression of health issues needing healing, each expanding my faith and understanding of God's healing power. There was the discovery of that gallstone while setting up the shop. Then the miraculous unrequested healing of my back, almost an added extra to God's rebuke as I judged the other worshippers.

## Spiritual Gifts and Healing

I received another unrequested healing when attending a course called Growth in the Spirit. Weeks of learning about the power of the Holy Spirit, the fruit, and the gifts culminated in a special service with the laying on of hands and prayer for the infilling and empowerment of the Holy Spirit.

As I read the lists of spiritual gifts in 1 Corinthians 12 (NIV), I was drawn to the word *service* in verse five—"different kinds of service but one Lord". I would ask the Lord to give me "power for service", nothing specific, not prophecy or miracles, nothing flashy and not tongues! I was wary of speaking in tongues—not sure of their value to me as a Christian and not convinced that those I'd heard were legit. They often sounded gibberish, babbling, not a proper language.

On the night, as we knelt at the communion rail, hands

were laid on by the elders, with prayer. Beryl had been nominated to pray with me and began to pray for me in tongues. My spirit soared as I realised this was definitely not gibberish but a real language—Cymraeg, the Welsh language of my grandmother. I heard the word *cariad* so many times I was soon in floods of tears. Cariad means "my love" or "my darling".

Later, when I asked Beryl if she knew her tongue was Welsh, she said, "I only know that the tongue I prayed with you tonight was not my usual prayer language."

I was humbled, realising that God had blessed me, showing me that I am His much-loved child, His darling, even though I had told Him which gift He could and could not give me!

But wait, there's more. On that night, I was unaware of an unrequested healing taking place. The psoriasis I'd suffered with since the age of 10 had gone. It had never been continuous, just flaring up in different locations on my body at times of stress. It first appeared on my scalp and hairline when I was studying for the eleven-plus examination. Then, as a teen, trying to lose weight, the tell-tale red scaly patches appeared around my middle—no bikinis for me. Another time when I was struggling to breastfeed Ann, the lesions popped out on my left breast.

Many months passed after I received the infilling of the Holy Spirit before I realised there had been no more lesions on my body.

Praise you, Lord! As I sought a closer spiritual walk with You, you healed me.

## More Healings

Not all the healing miracles I have received have been as big as my back injury or as ugly as psoriasis or that gallstone! Most are the small niggly things, like a cold or painful joints, a sore throat or the start of a migraine. The "treatment" is the same—rebuke the condition in Jesus's powerful name above all names. Some conditions need regular rebuking and healing claimed, until—Alleluia!—all symptoms have disappeared. There have been some other biggies, among them an ovarian cyst, an abdominal mass, arthritis, and worn cartilage in my left knee joint.

A potential biggie on 12 August 2009, was well documented in my journal, with my thoughts and prayers:

> Last night, I discovered a lesion on my left breast close to the aureole—it looks very odd. I probably would have dismissed it as an insect bite if I was still in Africa, and if I had not received that email last week! One of those ones "send to all women" emails, warning of the dangers of a new type of breast cancer which starts as a small redness but spreads outwardly and inwardly, very, very quickly. I deleted the email as scaremongering and can't recall who sent it. But when that lesion appeared I remembered the warning and stopped to take a second look. I rebuked the inflamed cells in Jesus's name and prayed for healing of the lesion; claimed Isaiah 53:5 (KJV), "By His stripes we *are* healed."

But then came the doubts. *Is this my time?* Something *will* polish me off eventually. Psalm 90: 10 (NIV) tells us, "The length of our days of our years is seventy years, or eighty if we have the strength." And I have passed seventy! Was I ready to go on that final exciting journey to everlasting life with my Lord? Was this a wakeup call? What did I still need to do to get myself spiritually prepared? And what about leaving? What must be done before then so there would not be a mess left behind?

So, I made a list. Journal entry for 12 August 2009 continues, " Need to make a new will and do much clearing out of stuff and decide *how* to spend the rest of my life— whether it is long or short."

The word I felt God giving me was to be *intentional* in all that I do. I called my doctor's surgery—no appointment available today and doctor going away Thursday until Monday. I decided to wait until next Monday and see Dr Nick, not the offered locum.

Next journal entry, Saturday, 15 August 2009: "*Thank you, Lord.* The lesion disappeared yesterday, gradually became lighter and now completely gone—just see the faintest pink where it was, but nothing more."

I sincerely thanked the Lord. I was grateful for the reprieve. My mother had died of breast cancer, but, "By His stripes I am healed." Whether it was just a spot or worse, it was all the same to Jesus. He wanted me whole and trusting Him!

## There is a Miracle in Your Mouth

And it was not all about me. Members of our home group were devastated when Jan was diagnosed with an aggressive cancer. The prognosis was horrendous—just weeks, maybe months! Jan attended the Sunday healing service but felt the people who prayed with her seemed to be praying for her to pass away peacefully without pain.

She was angry and felt cheated. "I want to see my girls graduate," she said, "and see them married." Her lovely daughters were 12 and 13 at the time. Our group agreed we would all pray for her healing, to be there for her girls. We asked the Lord to show us how to pray.

When Brian and I arrived home, there was a book on our divider—*There Is a Miracle in Your Mouth* by John Osteen. We had never seen or heard of this book and had no idea where it came from. It looked brand new—no name inside. We started to read. The essence of the book's teaching was not only to know, believe, and stand on God's word but to also *speak* the word. We were not just to think positively but to know God's promises and *speak* them out. "Death and life are in the power of the tongue" (Proverbs 18:21, NKJV).

The book was passed around to others in the group. We continued to pray with and for Jan, through all tests, gruelling treatments, and whatever came next. The word *cured* was never given, but there were periods of remission, and the original prognosis of weeks or months stretched to years. Both girls graduated. Fee met the man in her life, and Jan helped plan the wedding.

One morning, I drove over for a cuppa with Jan. Handing me a bag of clothing, she said, "I have been clearing out, and I think these will fit you. Too big for me now."

There were lovely blouses in the bag, one brand new! I was thanking her when the truth hit me. "What are you really doing?" I asked.

Jan chuckled "You have seen through me. I want to get everything sorted. I think my time is coming." She sounded so matter of fact. Ready to go home!

*Marie Bishop*

## God's Promises

Standing with Jan was a life-changing experience for me in knowing God's word, which is chock-a-block full of promises. There is a word for every situation we find ourselves in.

On those nights when sleep will not come, I remind God of the promise in Psalms 127:2 (NIV) "For He grants sleep to those He loves." And I know He loves me. Works better than any sleeping pill!

Nehemiah 8:10 (NIV) affirms, "The Joy of the Lord is my Strength." When feeling weighed down and overtired I declare this—sometimes by singing the old chorus. Saying, "I am so tired," just adds to the tiredness!

Declaring Philippians 4:13 (NKJV), "I can do all things through Christ who strengthens me," gives me the oomph I need. It might take me a bit longer than other younger, fitter models, but I *can* do it with Jesus's help!

I am uplifted and encouraged when weary or just feeling my age by Isaiah 40:31 (NIV): "Those who hope in the Lord will renew their strength. They will soar on wings like eagles, they will run and not grow weary, they will walk and not be faint."

## Be Anxious for Nothing

*Anxiety* appears to be today's buzz word; accepted as an inevitable part of everyday life, even though God's word commands us not to fear or be anxious. I recently read that "fear not" is mentioned 365 times in the Bible—one for every day of the year! Paul even gives the antidote in Philippians: "Do not be anxious for *anything* but in *everything*, by prayer and petition, *with thanksgiving*, present your requests to God.

154

And the Peace of God, which transcends *all* understanding will guard your hearts and minds in Christ Jesus" (Philippians 4:6–7, NIV, .

This was my school Bible passage back in the '50s, when my hometown, Liverpool, was recovering from the devastation of World War II. Piles of rubble were stark reminders of homes destroyed by Hitler's bombs. The Philippians 4 passage was printed and hung on classroom walls and read at every special assembly.

## Rooted and Grounded in God's Word

School days no longer start with Bible reading and prayer at assembly. For many children, God is shut out of their lives. This generation of children is nurtured as two-part entities, instead of the three-part beings God created them to be. Most receive excellent care for the body and soul. But for many children, the spirit, the part that lasts forever, is deprived and starved.

Is failure to develop spiritually the reason for the increase in depression today? Let's be honest, we all have times when we are sad, despondent, or even heartbroken. It could be when a relationship breaks down or someone we love dies or we lose our job or smash the car. That is not a disease; that is an emotional response. But it can lead to mental disease if we remain there.

God's Word gives us specific instruction on how to deal with this emotional response:

- "Do not let your hearts be troubled. Trust in God, trust also in me." (John 14:1, NIV)
- "As a man thinketh in his heart, so is he." (Proverbs 23:7, NKJV)

155

- "We take captive every thought to make it obedient to Christ." (2 Corinthians 10:5, NIV)
- "Give thanks in all circumstances." (1 Thessalonians 5:18, NIV)

There is always something to give thanks for, even in the worst of circumstances. Giving thanks gets rid of the "poor-me" attitude.

Knowing God's way is not hard; He has given us the Bible, the manufacturer's manual filled with His promises and instructions. Jesus condensed the first four commandments into one: "Love the Lord your God with all your heart, and all your soul, and with all your strength, and with all your mind, and love your neighbour as yourself" (Luke 10:27, NIV). That is still a command not a suggestion. There have been times when I haven't spoken to Him at all during the day. Is this the way I show love?

Knowing that God heals has been a major part of my spiritual journey. Some healings were the answer to my own prayers or the prayers of others, and some were a precious unrequested gift from my Abba. Each one has taught me a lesson, brought me closer to my Lord, and strengthened my faith.

# TWENTY

# A Time to Speak

## Come and Look at This!

"Brian! Come quickly."

Brian found me staring at the TV screen. The programme was a local current affairs show, a young man named Darren M was being interviewed. The name was familiar to us; we had heard a lot about Darren from my friend Hazel but had never met him or even seen him before. He was Hazel's boss, the manager of a Harare hotel. She liked Darren as a person, admired him as a hotelier, and was delighted when he was chosen to head the Hospitality Association at the young age of thirty-one.

The interview was in connection with his new role, and we watched an impressive young man—good-looking, confident, self-assured—as he shared his plans for putting Zimbabwe on the tourism map. But it was not Darren M, head hotel honcho or Hazel's boss that I was calling Brian to see. It was Darren's facial expression—a certain mannerism so familiar to us we could be looking at our own son, Craig! He effected a sort of downturn to the mouth while, at the same time, widening his

157

eyes and raising his eyebrows as he considered a question from the interviewer. This grimace, coupled with his surname hit me like a ton of bricks.

Our son's birth surname was the same as Darren's.

Craig's adoption had never been a secret; he'd grown up knowing he was "chosen". The arrival of cousin Paul when we were on holiday in England gave a practical demonstration of adoption and opened the way for questions and discussion. Craig was nine then. During his growing years, Craig had never expressed any interest in his birth parents. Meeting Karen was the trigger point; wanting to share the future with her and have a family of their own meant he wanted to know what was in the mix.

## Starting the Search

On a trip home to Zimbabwe from New Zealand, Craig confided to his sister, Ann, that he had been to the social welfare office in Harare hoping for information about his birth parents but had hit a brick wall. The law in Zimbabwe was closed adoption, the files firmly sealed, and he was turned away. Craig does not take no for an easy answer and was thinking of ways around the law, feeling very frustrated. Ann suggested he "speak to Mum", as she felt sure I had some knowledge. She was right. I did—not a lot but a vital piece of the puzzle.

On the day of Craig's adoption hearing, we had grouped around a typical government office table. I was seated at the top end to the left of the magistrate, Mr J. E.T. Harris, who was at the head. Brian was on my left. I held our precious baby. Mrs S, our case officer, was seated across the table from us. Craig was 7 weeks old and a little fractious. I was anxious and fussing. (If I could not settle him, would they take him away?) Those sentiments were not spoken words, but my actions said as much.

Mr Harris had a constant twinkle in his eye as though this hearing was a fun event—he was as relaxed as I was tense. The pages of the adoption document were stapled at the top left-hand corner, and as he turned each page, it landed squarely in front of me, revealing all the protected information. I read my baby's birth name with shock—knowing I should not know this. As I glanced furtively at J. E. T. Harris, he winked! Was it his intention that we should know the name? The documents were soon signed and witnessed, the hearing was over, and this beautiful baby boy was now legally *our* son, Craig Edward Paul Bishop. I stored away the knowledge that his name had ever been anything else.

From the outset, I believed our selection as Craig's adoptive parents had been God's plan. We were well down the list and had been told only in May that we would be parents within a year—not the following month! There were many reasons those couples ahead of us missed out. Several were away on overseas holidays. Some had wanted daughters. And then there were those who did not "fit the match". Social welfare matched backgrounds as closely as possible.

When we were blessed with our daughter, Ann, their colouring was so similar no one questioned that they were brother and sister. My dad and my brother Stuart have hazel-green eyes, and Craig's eyes started to darken at a year old from blue to that exact shade. Craig even has the same blood type as Ann and me. Whatever the reason for our jumping the queue, we felt that God intended Craig to be our son.

When Craig told me he wanted to know about his birth parents, I shared the little I knew—the surname—and suggested we go through the phone directory and ring every

M—— in the book. But he and Karen were flying back to New Zealand the following day, and so he decided to leave the search until the next time they visited Zimbabwe.

## Prayer for a Grandchild

Craig was happily settled into his new life in New Zealand with Karen. They had bought a cottage on seven acres, a selection of hens and a small flock of sheep—a mini farm! They shared a love of riding, exercised their kind neighbour's horse, and embarked on extending the cottage. Craig sounded happy whenever we spoke, but I had one concern. Karen had hinted babies may not be possible for her, and a child of his own would be vital for Craig, his own bloodline. One of my friends had similar concerns for her son, who was living with his girlfriend in England. We covenanted to pray for both of our boys to have children, praying for their children by name. I prayed for my grandson Paul.

The night Craig telephoned with the news is one I will never forget.

"Mum." he sounded serious. "Karen is pregnant. We are going to have a baby."

"What?" I shouted. "Did I hear right? Say again."

"Karen is going to have a baby. She is four months pregnant!"

"Four months already? Why didn't you tell us earlier?" I asked. Was he unhappy about this baby?

"We only found out yesterday. Karen went to the doctor for something else, and he did a test."

"Woohoo!" I whooped down the party line. "That is wonderful, son. Here's your dad. Tell him the good news."

I handed the phone to Brian. He spoke, quieter than me and

at length, assuring Craig we were delighted to be grandparents. I heard him say, "Your mother is doing cartwheels around the lounge."

Not quite, but I was dancing and praising God. My prayer had been answered. Craig would be a father! I took the phone back from Brian.

"Are you really okay with this, Mum?" he asked.

"I am delighted, Craig. This is an answer to my prayer! And what's more, I know that you're having a son, and I know what you'll call him."

He probably relegated his mother to the crazy basket at this point in the conversation but replied, "We haven't even thought about names yet. Karen will be having a scan soon to check that everything is okay. Will let you know."

"Craig," I called out before he could ring off, "will you get married?"

"Yeah! Of course! But not until after the baby is born." No rush then.

On the day of the scan, Craig called me at work.

"You were right, Mum. The baby is a boy, due at the end of March. Good guess. You couldn't know for certain."

I reminded him of my prayers for him to have a child of his own and that I had been praying for my grandson by name. "I know what you will call him!"

"You can't possibly know that." He said, sounding scornful. "We haven't decided yet. Can't agree."

"What names are on the list?" I asked.

"Karen likes Benjamin. I like Joel, but that would probably become Joe. Paul as a second name after me and Karen's dad."

"That's the one," I said. "I have been praying for Paul."

Benjamin Joel Paul arrived five weeks early on 21 February,1995.

The wedding date was set for 20 November. Brian and I

travelled to New Zealand for seven memorable weeks, getting to know both our new daughter and grandson. They were all at the airport to meet us. Ben was seven months old, a gorgeous, happy, and contented baby. Ben's christening was to be in the same service as the wedding; their minister had refused to christen Ben until his parents were married! Brian and I had Ben to ourselves while Karen and Craig had a short honeymoon, and we prayed our own blessing over him.

The arrival of Benjamin, the wedding, and our New Zealand trip, pushed any thought of finding Craig's birth parents out of our minds, onto the back-burner. And there it remained—until that TV programme and Darren M's facial expression, grimacing just like Craig! Again, I stored the information away and planned that, on his next visit to Zimbabwe, we could get Craig and Darren together and see where that led.

## Can it Be?

Then Hazel had told me her boss would soon be leaving Zimbabwe. So I knew the time was now, or we'd lose the only lead we had. An appointment with Darren was arranged, and I presented myself at his office, not sure how I was going to broach the subject. He is naturally a very charming man and was warm and welcoming. He asked about Ann, also in hotel management but was obviously wondering why I was there. Hazel had given no clue.

When I told him I'd come to discuss my son, Craig, he looked puzzled, trying to recall meeting him. As I shared the story, he hung onto my words, rapt, as I told him about Craig, the surname on the document, and the date of birth and finished by asking if Craig could be his brother.

Every emotion had shown on his face as I spoke, and he was visibly moved when I gave him the selection of photographs taken over the years—Craig with Ann as tots, family gatherings, school sports, holidays, sailing with Brian. Each photograph was studied, looked at more than once, and many questions were asked. Then he said, with feeling, "I wish my life had been more like Craig's!"

He shared his side of the story. Darren had never known why he and his sister Andrea had been placed in the Rhodesia Children's Home at the ages of 3 and 5. They stayed there for almost a year and then were taken back by their mother to Mutare, where their father and grandparents lived. His parents divorced shortly after, and Darren and Andrea moved to Harare with their mother. Sarah remarried, moved to South Africa, and had two more children with her second husband. Darren's school holidays were spent with his own father, Frank M. But he grew up feeling confused. He was clearly intrigued to know he had another brother.

Where to from here? My aim was to make contact with Craig's birth mother, Darren's mother, who was living in South Africa. He sensitively proposed a plan to give the photographs and my covering letter to a friend and ask her to pass this information on to Sarah. This would lessen his mother's shock and embarrassment that her son knew all her secrets. So started a time of waiting—but not for long!

## Contact with Sarah

The letter from Sarah arrived two weeks later. She shared her heartache at never holding her baby or even seeing him, leaving the hospital after two days, empty. She thought often of the baby she had given away, hoping her decision had been the right one, that he was happy, but with no way of knowing! The photographs and letter from me with details of his family had given her assurance and healed some of the hurt.

My own feelings were strange. At no time did I feel threatened but more as though my own family had been enlarged, like researching DNA and a family tree. Craig was already living his own life in New Zealand. Maybe I would have felt threatened by his birth mother when he was a young boy, but now I enjoyed sharing snippets of his life with Sarah. For me, there was a real awareness that all children are gifts from God, for a season, loaned not owned.

Five years passed before Craig and Karen returned to Zimbabwe, this time bringing Ben with them. The year was 2000, the millennium, with all the uncertainty that brought. We had planned a family celebration, seeing in the new year sailing in the houseboat *Shambira* on Lake Kariba, followed by a week in Inyanga. This was a memorably, happy time, especially seeing Ben and Jono interacting as cousins and fussing tiny Meghan.

Their return flight home to New Zealand was routed through Cape Town, allowing Craig to meet his birth mother. The venue chosen was a neutral one, Kirstenbosch Gardens. Karen said she recognised Sarah as looking similar to me—same colouring but trimmer. Ben was intrigued to now have three grandmas! Sarah and Craig spent a day together—questions asked and answered, feelings explored and expressed. This was healing for Craig. I hope it was for Sarah too.

But, what about all those coincidences?

Were they just coincidences or were the *Godincidences*?

There was my "random" viewing of that TV interview with Darren, whose surname was the same as Craig's birth surname—and the fact I'd recognised their shared facial expression.

And he "just happened" to be my friend's boss—allowing her to tell me when he was moving out of our orbit and arrange a meeting before he left?

And then there was that wink from the adoption magistrate, J. E. T. Harris when the documents were "accidentally" turned before me, revealing Craig's birth name. It was confusing at the time but made sense years later when Sarah told me Craig's birth father was named Harris. Were they related? Did that explain the wink?

And the fact that Sarah's parents were *missionaries*. Were they praying for a Christian adoptive family for their grandchild? Is that why we jumped the queue? I don't know the answers, but Brian and I knew from day one.

Craig was God's gift to us.

*NB. Some names in this chapter have been changed for privacy.*

# TWENTY-ONE

# A Time to Rejoice

**Empty Nesters**

An unexpected season started for Brian and me when Katie became our foster daughter.

In 1989, we were almost empty nesters. Craig was in New Zealand. Ann was still at home, working at Meikles and planning to move into a flat with friends. Fay and Gail were both married, Gail living in Bulawayo with husband and three children.

Each year Gail and the children spent Christmas with their favourite Auntie Fay. Videos taken of these visits revealed that Katie, at 7, was not talking. Tina, 4 years younger, chatted away, but Katie would just give affirming noises, no words. Gail insisted there was no problem, that Katie talked a lot at home but was shy outside her immediate family. The following Christmas, Fay was intentional, speaking directly to Katie, trying to draw her into conversation, with little success. Something was very wrong.

## Medical checks

Fay and I travelled together to Bulawayo, hoping to find the cause. The first appointment was with her GP, to check if there was anything physical that needed correcting. The lady doctor, wary at first, eventually opened up with her concerns. Unexplained injuries were on her records—sprained ankle, painful wrist and elbow, plus bruises. Katie's hearing was good, and there was no physical reason why she was not forming words. The doctor referred us to a paediatrician at KG 6 Centre for children with disabilities, securing a consultation that afternoon.

After introducing ourselves and sharing our concerns, we sat in the waiting room while the lovely paediatrician took Katie into her office to observe her at play. Model school rooms and doll's houses were used, with a selection of miniature dolls to choose from. Questions were asked and scenarios suggested. Katie needed to place the dolls in appropriate situations for these scenarios—thus revealing her life experiences non-verbally.

When the exercise was completed, Katie was left in the play room while Fay and I received the results. Her positioning of the dolls revealed sexual abuse, although the abuser was not clearly identified. Dr T said that Katie, at eight, was aware of right and wrong, and therefore, some of her responses were guarded. She recommended Katie be removed from both her home and the school, where she was the only non-Ndebele speaker.

## Planning

We went back to the flat to discuss this life changer with Gail. Fay suggested that Katie live with her and Bill during term time, attend the local school, and go home to her parents for holidays, like a boarding school. Gail needed to discuss these plans with Theo, and Fay would need Bill's confirmation. We headed home to tackle the task of finding a place at a local school.

Belvedere Junior School, closest to Fay and Bill, was first choice, but they had a long waiting list. We decided to apply to every government school in both of our school zones; surely there would be a place somewhere! I applied to Borrowdale, where our children had been students, as well as Vainona Junior and the new Greystone Park Primary School, falsely giving our address as Katie's home address.

All responses were negative, until, in September, a place was offered by Greystone Park Primary School for the following year. It wasn't ideal, but no other places were offered. We made a plan. Fay would drop her off at school in the morning with her bike; Gabriel would cycle there at one o'clock and ride to our home with her. Katie could do her homework under Loveness's supervision until Fay collected her later in the afternoon. It wasn't what we'd hoped for, but we agreed to give it a good go.

## Change of Plan

Then came the bombshell. Bill felt unable to commit to taking on Katie permanently. He had always been such a fun-loving uncle to all the children in the family, but the prospect of being *in loco parentis* was too much. Fay came to our house in a floods of tears, wracked with a confusion of emotions. And she felt a sense of loss. Fay had been looking forward to being a stand-in mum, having a child in her care.

"What can we do now?" Fay wept. "She can't stay there in that school."

Brian put his arm around Fay. "She can come and stay here. Craig's room is empty."

"Are you sure?" I asked. "You're older than Bill. Are you okay with another child?"

"She's just a little girl," he said. "We've had a few of those!"

So, we accepted the place at Greystone Park School, and Katie became our foster daughter, starting the unexpected season for Brian and me. Ann put her plan to move into a flat with friends on hold; she would stay and be a big sister to Katie! Our home group were, mostly, encouraging. Hilda was the exception; widowed with a headstrong son, she thought we were quite mad. Were we? Perhaps it would only be for a short time. By the time Belvedere School had a place, maybe Bill would be ready to be a stand-in dad.

An appointment was made for Katie to meet the principal and see her new school before term ended. Miss Cooper chatted in a friendly welcoming manner to her new pupil, trying to assess her abilities, if she was special needs. But Katie clung to me and kept her head buried in my side for the entire time. Miss Cooper agreed to enrol her, recommending the smallest class in her year group, so she would have more focussed attention.

After Christmas, Katie happily settled into her own bedroom in our house. We had a glimmer of hope on her arrival at our home when she shouted the words, "Hamba," and, "Voetsak," to our big black Labrador as he came to the car to welcome her. Her vocal cords were working after all.

During the January holidays Katie had met children at Sunday school and planned to start Brownies with a girl in our road. They were all invited to her ninth birthday party at the end of January. I made a new dress for the occasion, and Fay baked a cake shaped like a butterfly. Brian and Ann organised a treasure hunt, Katie enjoying the fun, smiling, and laughing for the whole afternoon. This changed when she became the centre of attention as everyone sang "Happy Birthday" and she saw the mountain of gifts. She covered her face with her hands and dissolved into tears! It was all too much. This was her first ever birthday party.

## New School

By the time school started in early February, she was settling into her new life and showing increased confidence. There were still very few words coming from her mouth but no signs of anxiety or distress at starting a new school. Her class teacher welcomed her warmly, and I headed home feeling like a new mum.

I had taken leave from work in case I was called to the school, but the telephone remained silent. Greystone Park teachers were very caring; I learned later that they prayed for her and other students at their staff meetings, not usual practice for government schools. This put all the changes into perspective:was Greystone Park School and our home God's plan for Katie all along? She loved her church family at Christchurch Borrowdale and later wrote that Sunday was her "best day"!

One of the first school events of the year was Interhouse Sports Day. Katie was not competing, and her teacher (Mrs K) kept her close. As they were watching a relay race, suddenly there was this loud shout, "Go, go, go, go!"

Mrs K looked down in disbelief at the little blonde girl animatedly jumping up and down at her side shouting words in the excitement of the race—breakthrough!

Her speech improved with training from her speech therapist, Mrs McLoed, and she loved learning music. Recorders were part of the school curriculum, and she was soon incorporated into the church music group. Brownies on Friday afternoons were a highlight, and her sights were set on camp. We gently told her this could be a problem because of bed wetting—no pressure, but we started to pray about this. On Sunday mornings, she would head for the prayer team in the Lady chapel to pray for healing.

## Prayer for Deliverance

Another area of concern were the night terrors; she would wake us in the night with horrible choking, coughing sounds, her face red and contorted but still asleep.

One episode of *The 700 Club* covered deliverance in children, and the name of a local person flashed on the screen. I booked an appointment. She gave me sound advice, which I shared with Brian, and we started a programme of praying for Katie while she slept, binding and rebuking Satan in Jesus's name, sometimes beside her bed but often with our hands placed on the lounge wall that backed onto her bedroom. There was no lightning deliverance, but gradually the choking/coughing stopped, and so did the bedwetting. Just in time for Brownie camp! One Sunday evening, when she was 11, she said she wanted to ask Jesus to come into her heart. We knelt at her bedside and prayed together.

As she approached the end of her primary school years and Brian and were discussing where to next, my bosses, Ken and Ian, added an additional "perk" to my portfolio, payment for private school fees. We were able to register her for Gateway High School, our first choice, ideally situated en route to my work, close to Brian's workshop, and a Bible-based Christian school.

Greystone Park Primary School's prize-giving in December 1993 was a night of surprises. Craig and Ann had each won the top boy and top girl awards at the end of their primary years. But knowing how Katie struggled with learning, we were not expecting any accolades. When her name was called for the John Quincy Overcomers Cup, there were floods of tears and whoops of joy! Celebration dinner with Granny Chris and all of Katie's family that night.

## Wedding of the Year!

Ann and Nick's wedding on Easter Monday, was a time of great excitement for us all, and a milestone for Katie. She and Saskia were first-time bridesmaids, wearing floral dresses of yellow, white and pink! Material for Ann's dress was bought in Johannesburg and prayed over before cutting. The photos say it all! Ann was a beautiful Bride -and the day one of joy and celebration.

## New School, Steps of Faith

Gateway Christian School opened up more musical opportunities. The school orchestra hired instruments to students, and Katie was allocated a clarinet. Uncle Brian played the cornet, which meant they could read the same music for their B-flat instruments! And they enjoyed lovely times of practicing together and playing in the church's music group.

In January 1995, James Martin, our parish priest and friend, approached us with the news that Katie had signed herself up for confirmation later in the year. Brian was concerned that she was just following the crowd so asked Pauline to monitor her to ensure she was making a genuine decision for Christ. Her confirmation day would be on 18 November, the same day as Craig and Karen's wedding. Brian and I were leaving Katie with Ann and Nick as we headed off to New Zealand for the wedding, sad to be missing such a milestone in her life but confident Gail, Fay, Tina, Ann, Nick, and the rest of the family would be there to support her and pray for her. I sewed her white confirmation dress and reminded everyone to take lots of photographs.

## Trip Down Under

Brian and I started our holiday in Perth with our niece Lee; her husband, Evan; and their two lovely children, Leesa, two, and Jacob, ten days old! Five days of making memories, seeing the sights, and catching up with our Pebworth Place neighbours, the Burnetts. Then on 10 October, we flew to Auckland, where Craig, Karen, and 7-month-old Ben, were waiting at the airport to welcome us. This was the baby I had prayed for by the name Paul before his conception; his full name is Benjamin Joel Paul! What a joy to hold him, play silly games, and hear his infectious giggle. And what a joy to experience life in the cottage on the "lifestyle block" Craig and Karen had bought north of Auckland. Five acres of land surrounded their cottage, two of the acres covered with protected native trees, with plenty of space for exotic chickens and a small flock of sheep.

A trip around the North Island before the wedding had been planned, a sort of extended honeymoon for the couple, which continued after the wedding with both sets of in-laws in tow! A motel at Paihia became our base for the first week, allowing us to explore the surrounding countryside, meet some of Craig and Karen's friends, and learn New Zealand history at Russell and Waitangi. We took a day trip to Cape Rienga via ninety-mile beach, where we slid down the dunes like kids!

A quick trip back home to check on chooks and sheep, and then we were on the road again, heading for Kawerau, where we'd be meeting with Karen's family. More mind-blowing experiences included volcanic activity as we visited Hot Water Beach, Rotorua, and witnessed White Island volcano blowing smoke. Life in New Zealand was revealed as very different to life in Africa.

We were back in Albany at the end of October to make final wedding arrangements. We attended church as a family at Devonport Presbyterian, where the ceremony would take place on 18November. There were trips to the city to see where Karen worked and visit art galleries and Kelly Tarlton's Sea Life Aquarium. Kelly Tarlton's was a visit to remember. In 1995, New Zealand hosted CHOGM, a milestone conference, as South Africa was welcomed back into the Commonwealth. Nelson Mandela, as president of South Africa, was the star of the show.

CHOGM was not in our thoughts as we headed for Kelly Tarlton's Aquarium, with Ben in his push chair. We stood looking at the fish tanks when there was a disturbance at the entrance. I nudged Brian and said, "That man looks very like Swithun Mombeshora. Do you recognise him?" He was the Zimbabwean minister of higher education who we had met several years ago when he visited Gwebi College.

Brian said, "Not sure but could be. I certainly recognise that man over there." He pointed behind me.

I turned and saw Robert Mugabe, surrounded by his guards, walking through the crowds towards the tunnels leading to the shark tanks. No one was giving him a second glance.

*This is ridiculous!* I thought. Here we are, fellow Zimbabweans, miles from home, by coincidence at the same tourist attraction. So I called out, "Excuse me, sir. Excuse me."

The people between us seemed to melt away as he turned towards this forward woman.

"I hope you are enjoying your New Zealand visit as much as I am, sir," I said, extending my hand.

RGM took my hand, looking slightly bewildered. "Indeed, yes," he said. "Are you from Zimbabwe?"

"From Harare," I replied. "Here for our son's wedding."

"Have a good time," he said as he was hustled forward by his henchmen.

Brian muttered in my ear, "All those years of army call-up I spent chasing him around the bush, and here you are, shaking his hand!"

I felt good about the interaction. He was our president after all, unknown and ignored by the crowd of tourists in Kelly Tarlton's.

His guards didn't hold the same view. They surrounded me, asking for my name and address. Naively, I thought this could lead to an invite to government house, but my protective son saw the questioning differently. He addressed the guards. "New Zealand is a free country," he said. "We are free to speak to our leaders in public." And he steered me away from them, muttering "Bunch of thugs. Who do they think they are?!"

No invitation to tea with the president was ever received, so maybe Craig was right. But I cherish the memory.

## Another Wedding of the year

That 18 November dawned gloriously sunny—perfect for a wedding day!

The whole day was glorious. Karen made a beautiful bride, surrounded by friends and family. There was an atmosphere of true joy. Janet held Ben during his parents' wedding ceremony and presented him to be christened after the service, wrapped in the family christening shawl brought from Zimbabwe for the occasion. Then came the dinner, speeches, and dancing—a fitting celebration.

Brian and I took Ben home to care for him, enabling Karen and Craig to have their special wedding night at a hotel. We had been surprised there was no water used by the minister for the infant baptism—so we used this opportunity to pray for Benjamin, anoint him, and sign him with the cross of Christ—claiming him for Jesus.

Sunday was gift opening day and relaxing time before the family headed back to the Bay of Plenty. Karen's folks stayed, and we took day trips together to Waiheke Island, Gulf Harbour, and across to the black sand of Muriwai.

Sadly, our time in New Zealand came to an end, and we headed home feeling torn. Would we ever see the new family members again? Little did we know that, before too long, we would become Kiwis too!

We turned our faces towards home, eager to hear what Katie had been doing with Ann and Nick.

# TWENTY-TWO

# A Time to Mourn

## The Loss of a Much-Loved Child

The New Year started on a positive note; we were still basking in the lovely memories of Craig and Karen's wedding and our first grandchild, Benjamin, when Ann and Nick announced in January that they were expecting a baby. Katie was moving forward on her faith journey and had signed up for the Scripture Union Camp in January. Our whole church was in revival mode as another Alpha course started. This course is designed to both introduce people to Jesus and strengthen faith of Christians. There was an air of expectation for exciting times ahead.

Then, in February 1996, our whole world was turned upside down when our beloved Katie died suddenly. There was no warning, no prolonged illness, no time to prepare. Losing a child is pain like no other.

Brian and I had returned Sunday night from an Alpha weekend away at Resthaven—a time of Great spiritual high. Katie had spent the weekend with her best friend, Antoinette, and not completed the project she needed to hand in on

Monday. Brian and I disagreed about this. He thought it was beyond her capability, but I was cross with her for not even trying. Somehow this escalated into an altercation and degenerated into a full-blown row—with me complaining about needing to work until I was sixty-five to keep Kate at a private school and she was not doing her stuff!

Thirty hours later, she died.

Katie was not feeling well when I collected her from school 4.30 p.m. Monday. I called our doctor, Gerry, who said it sounded like flu. He instructed me to give her plenty of fluids and bring her into the surgery at 8 a.m on Tuesday After supper, she was physically sick; could it be gastroenteritis? I cancelled Alpha group and helped Katie with a bath before bed.

She was restless all night, climbed into my bed and snuggled down for a while and then went back to her own, with her favourite worship music playing. We both dozed until she called out at 3.30 a.m., and I rushed to her room to find her collapsed, unconscious on the floor. The ambulance was called by pressing an emergency button. She was not breathing, so I started CPR—chest compressions and mouth to mouth. I grabbed a phone and called Jackman's number, shouting into the receiver on the floor and then carried on CPR until ambulance arrived. Brendon J jumped over the wall to unlock the gate for them to drive in. Paddles were used to start her heart again, and she was put on oxygen for the trip to the hospital. But I now believe that, when she called me at 3.30, she had died on the floor of her bedroom and was on her way to see Jesus, face to face.

Gail, Fay, Bill, Jean and Brian, and Ann and Nick were at the hospital too. We watched as the doctors worked to resuscitate her, to no avail. The machines were finally switched off.

Brendan had called Brian to tell him Katie was not well

and to come home as soon as possible. He turned into our drive as we all arrived back from the hospital—6 a.m., Tuesday, 20 February, the day before Benjamin's first birthday.

## Loving Support

I was numb, in shock—it all felt unreal as though a bad dream or something I was watching from the side-lines. All feelings were frozen; I was stunned.

Ingrid, Ann's friend came and set up quiet background music, scriptural music and made tea constantly for the streams of people flooding through the house. Ann's pastor, Ricky Decker, came to the house. He shared the scripture from Psalms 116:15 (NIV): "Precious in the sight of the Lord is the deaths of his saints.". Had I ever heard that scripture? What did it mean? And how could I process it into this tragedy? Did God weep with me?

Our doctor, Gerry, wept with us when we saw him later that day. He assumed that Katie had recovered from her sickness when we didn't keep the eight o'clock appointment. Then an MOH official arrived at his surgery to collect her medical records and told him their suspicions. The autopsy revealed the cause of death to be Waterhouse-Friedrichsen syndrome of meningitis. Where had she contracted this? It was a mystery to our medical friends—a very rare strain, hardly ever seen in Zimbabwe. There was no meningococcal vaccine in 1996, so all the children in the orchestra, the choir, her class, and GP youth group were classed as "at risk" and needed gamma globulin to hold back an epidemic.

This was a time of deep despair and wonderful support from so many people. Donna, a friend from church who was a nurse, bought a new medical journal that gave up-to-date information about the disease as "causing death in minutes or hours". She wanted to assure me that it was not my neglect that had taken Katie from us. Friends, family, neighbours, pastors, and teachers all came to share in the shock and the grieving. The children from school were shaken—one moment Katie was playing her clarinet at orchestra practice, and the next she had died.

There are no notes in my journal for the days leading up to the funeral on 23 Friday. But on that day the anguish of my remorse is recorded:

> Lord please forgive my idle unproductive, destructive words.
> Father if I could change things and have her back, I would willingly work until 90, just to see her grow into a fully blossomed young woman of God!

That night I sobbed myself to sleep again but awoke with a song in my head, **"Blessed Be the Name of the Lord"**:

> The name of the Lord is a strong tower.
> The righteous run into it, and they are saved!

Those words were so comforting—even though I could not claim to be righteous.

The Bible reading for that morning was Matthew 21:28–32.

Notes in my journal read, "This passage reminds me that God knows what is in my heart and heeds that more than the words on my lips, and He forgives me."

The following day, Saturday, 24 February 1996, was recorded as "a down and up day" a "try to get back to normal day". We had so much support from wonderful friends and neighbours. Jean insisted we have our Saturday morning walk as we usually did, both weeping most of the way; what a blessing Jean is! Visits came from neighbours on both sides, Molly in the morning. I was on a crying jag when Sylvia and Wonder came in the afternoon. I just wanted to hide but they are such a caring, devout Catholic couple, whose love surrounded us, as they prayed with us. Fay and Bill had brought lunch, and Mandy and Ken visited—lovely encouraging words from Mandy.

## Reviewing

Brian wanted to go over every moment of Katie's last day, moment by moment. She had waved to him, smiling, as he drove off early Monday morning. And when he returned twenty-four hours later, she was gone. He wanted my assurance she was loved; he suspected I had been impatient with her. I had often been strict with her.

I journaled:

> Please forgive me, Lord, for the times I was too hard on her. I have to change through all this suffering. Lord, please change me."

Then:

> Thank You, Heavenly Father, for the tangible feeling of peace that flooded me while I was in the bath, truly beyond all earthly understanding.

Thank You too, Lord, that Brian and I were able to talk openly—that we could reaffirm that our Katie is alive and is with You.

## Journaling

Journal entries from the weeks that followed record the progression of my grief:

*Sunday, 25 February*

New every morning is His Love, not just tears and heartache! Song, "Come into His Presence with Thanksgiving in My Heart" assures me I am loved, but I also feel that I have been chastened, disciplined. The times that I have spoken words I don't mean or believe remind me that I will one day stand before God and have to account for every idle, non-productive word. My tongue has been a problem for a very long time. "Lord, I want to change!"

*Monday, 26 February*

A hard day for Brian. I feel tired, drained and have a severe backache. Dr Gerry visited and took blood test for meningitis. Giving Kate CPR could have infected me. Prayer for healing:

Please, Lord, spare me and heal me!
Brian, Craig, and Ann could not stand
it if I had the illness too.

I awakened from a sleep, with revelation,
knowing the cause of the pain was *not*
meningitis! Gerry was unaware of the huge
gallstone sitting inside me. His partner, Joe,
had been my GP during that diagnosis. In
the morning, I called Gerry and asked if
all the trauma could have caused a flare-up.
He confirmed that, if my insides look like
my tear-ravaged face, there would be severe
inflammation.

No meningitis developed. PTL

*28 February 1996*

Awoke to praise instead of tears today—*Great
is thy Faithfulness Lord unto me!* running
through my mind.

The reading for the day was the doxology in Romans
11:33–36. God is all-knowing and wise. Thoughts in my
journal continued:

God's decision to allow Katie to go to Him
early is beyond my understanding! But God
*knew* all the circumstances; I was on my
own, and Brian also alone working at Klein
Kopjes. God chose not to answer my prayer
for healing, restoring Katie to carry on life on
earth, but He gently took her at 3.30 a.m. By

the time the machines were switched off and the hospital doctor declared her dead, she had been with Jesus for two hours! No way would she have wanted to come back.

I Praise You, Lord, even in these circumstances. You gave me "strength for today" and even "bright hope for tomorrow". Your faithfulness is great, indeed! Thank you too, Father, for the assurance that she had received Jesus as her Lord and Saviour and could go straight to You.

By Sunday, 3 March, two weeks had passed since the Alpha Holy Spirit weekend and twelve days since Katie died. I listened to Mark Taylor on the radio talking about trials and tribulations *strengthening* our faith!? He quoted Roman 8:28 (NKJV): "*All* things work together for good for those who love the Lord; to those who are called according to His purposes." Mark said, we ask the Lord to enlarge and strengthen our faith and then complain that He allows the trials and tribulations that make our faith grow! My cry from the heart, "Lord, will we come out of this terrible time stronger in faith? I hope so!"

On 13 March, the WFT daily reading was Psalm 37:25–26, "The Lord never forsakes those who love Him."

## Mother's Day

On 12 May, Mother's Day, there was much sadness and weeping! And resentment—how could God allow this to happen? My journal entry: "Why did Katie die?"

184

I don't believe that it was God's will that she should contract meningitis and die at fifteen, especially when she was making good progress at school, in friendships, and in her spiritual life. The future was looking good! I believe that disease is the work of Satan. Humankind allowed disease to come into the world when they listened to the devil in the Garden of Eden.

*But* Jesus said, "Take heart, I have overcome the world" (John 16:33 NIV).

So, why did Katie, a child of God, get sick and die so rapidly?

I listed the circumstances, trying to make sense of this tragedy:

1. It was my practise to pray for her, and my whole family, daily. Did I forget on that Monday? I certainly prayed for her during the night, but was I praying just for her comfort and not beseeching God for healing? Could be, because I had no idea she was so ill! Did God shield me from the truth of her illness, or did I miss the prompting of the Holy Spirit?
2. Was it my complaining about having to work for years ahead to cover the school fees?
3. Katie herself had missed two Sundays at church; was she a bit out of touch with God?
4. We had spent the weekend praying to receive the infilling of the Holy Spirit on the Alpha weekend away. Did this generate interest from the devil?
5. Brian had felt a demonic presence at Klein Kopjes during the night of Monday and had laughed at the devil.

No answers or explanations. Back to trusting God was in control.

The journal entries throughout the year continue with many heart cries to God.

## End of 1996

Here are my thoughts recorded at the end of 1996 (27 December):

> The main lessons I have learned during this most painful time:
>
> 1. To *trust* in the Lord with all my heart and lean not on your own understanding
> 2. *Nothing* can separate me from the love of God through Christ Jesus—death can't; life can't
> 3. To give thanks *in* all circumstances
> 4. The *blessing* of Christian love and fellowship— *suffering* can equip us to help others who are suffering to become Jesus's hands and feet
>
> Thank You, Lord, for your love and patience as I learn to trust You completely.
>
> Thank You for the gift of scriptural songs to fill my mind when I awake during the darkest times.
>
> Thank you for the love and support from family and friends.
>
> Thank you, Father God, for giving Katie to us for six years. During this time, she came

to know Jesus as her Lord and Saviour and to experience Your love through the body of Christ, her Christchurch family whom she loved.

Thank you, Lord, for the assurance that we will meet again when the trumpet sounds.

Adjusting to life without Katie was a daily decision. Some things were just too hard, like driving past her school as parents were collecting their children. I plotted another route home. Sitting in the music group at church next to the youth orchestra where she had played recorder and clarinet brought floods of tears. It was easier to sit in the main body of the church until I could sing again.

The sense of emptiness was all-consuming. And guilt—she was with me, in my care, so how come this had happened? And then there was depression. Dr Gerry recommended I work through this, one day at a time, weeping when I needed to weep, writing down thoughts, not relying on medication. Those journaled thoughts, questions, and complaints became prayers.

Each day was moment by moment, talking to God.

# TWENTY-THREE

# A Time to Let Go

### New Grandson

The glimmer of light in that dark tunnel was anticipating the birth of a grandchild. Ann and Nick's first child was due in August 1996, so I created a selection of jerseys from newborn size to 6 months. Knitting became my number one pastime. At times I felt like Charles Dickens's Madame Defarge! The scans all looked good and reassuring that all was well with the precious boy. His arrival was eagerly anticipated.

Early Sunday morning, 11 August, Nick telephoned, his voice controlled. "Hi, Ma, just wanted to let you know we are on our way."

Ann had started contractions the previous evening; they'd been getting stronger through the night until they were very strong and coming at regular intervals. Nick was in charge of the timing! They were heading for the Avenues Clinic. Brian and I were ready for church early, hovering close to the phone waiting to hear that all was well.

At nine o'clock, Nick phoned again to tell us that Jonathan had been born at eight thirty. Jonathan was perfect, Ann was exhausted, but both were well! Our church family joined us in praising the Lord for his precious gift of a grandson. As soon as the service ended, we headed into town to meet Jonathan Anthony Simcoe Read.

Cuddling a baby is always comforting, and new life helped with the healing process. Daily, I would call in to see Ann and baby Jonathan after work. Brian often popped in for morning tea. Jono's milestones became ours as our lives settled into a new pattern. That first Christmas with a baby grandson was a memorable one. The combined Bishop/Read clan assembled at our house, plus some friends, all showering gifts on Jonathan. His first birthday was a treasure hunt at the botanical gardens—babies in prams, friends and family picnicking under a wintery sun.

## Letting Go

The year had been very hard for Nick's mother, Marianne, who was battling cancer. She remained positive, presenting as a strong lady, stoically embracing chemotherapy as well as some natural cures. We joined her many friends and family in praying for her.

When Nicholas was offered a scholarship at University of Surrey for his master's degree, his mother was delighted, and encouraged him to take it and move to England despite her health struggle. This was the career path she and John had wanted for their son; Nick's early marriage had not been part of their plan, and this opportunity seven years later was too good to be missed.

But we all knew how much we would miss them. And when they left in August, the goodbyes at the airport were graunching. The future was uncertain for Marianne; she and

John were heading to South Africa to pursue a severe form of natural therapy, desperately hoping this would succeed in stopping the cancer.

She came home after three weeks of controlled fasting treatment, skin and bone, devastated when tests showed the cancer was still there. Another round of chemotherapy was scheduled for October, raising hope again.

When I visited after work they were standing in the doorway, clinging to each other, weeping uncontrollably. The oncologist had delivered devastating news—latest tests showed the cancer was still raging. He had declared there would be no more chemotherapy; this was only buying them days, maybe weeks! Shooting from the hip. This was the end of the journey. They were shocked, shaken, heartbroken, and without hope.

John asked if I would stay with Marianne while he drove to collect Saskia from her friend's house. I made tea while Marianne splashed her face and calmed down a little. We sat side by side on the couch.

"Can we pray together?" I asked Marianne.

She knew I had been praying for her throughout the illness, but this was the first time I had the opportunity to pray with her, face to face, just the two of us. Tears streamed down both of our faces as I prayed, asking God to reverse the doctor's prognosis, asking for healing, strength, peace—crying out for so many things.

I paused and asked Marianne, "Is there anything I have forgotten?"

She took deep breaths, bravely bringing her weeping under control—her eyes closed—and then said, "Please let me live longer to get to know You better." She was praying—asking God for more time. Marianne, praying to our Heavenly Father!

God answered her prayer and gave her more time. I never again had time alone with Marianne. She was always surrounded by her many loving friends and family. During those added fourteen weeks of life, Nick came home from the United Kingdom, bringing Ann and her precious grandson. Catherine also came home in November and had her wedding in the garden; Howard made the trip from Australia.

Nick needed to return to Uni to continue his degree course, flying back to England in early January but leaving Ann and Jonathan to stay on. Before he left for the airport, he asked his mother if he could pray for her. "Mum, the Bible tells us in James to ask the elders to pray for those who are sick. I know I am your son, but spiritually I am your elder, so may I pray for you?"

Marianne nodded tearfully, and Nick laid hands on her and prayed—a very moving moment. He left knowing he would not see his mother again.

A week later, Saskia was heading away to Germany as an exchange student. The flight from Africa to Europe was long and convoluting. The morning after she arrived, her exchange Mum dialled John and Marianne's home. It was around eight in the evening Zimbabwe time; Marianne was in bed, John reading in the chair beside her. She was able to speak with Saskia and know that her precious youngest child was safe and starting her year-long adventure.

When the call ended, she closed her eyes to sleep, John beside her reading the paper—until he looked up and saw that his darling wife had left him. She had gone on her final journey.

Were Marianne's prayers answered? God gave her extra time, but did she get to know Him in those days? God's word tells us in 2 Peter 3:9 that our loving Heavenly Father does not want one soul to be lost.

I know God loved Marianne and wanted her in His kingdom—and she turned towards Him in her darkest hours.

See you later, sister!

# TWENTY-FOUR

# A Time to Dance

Solomon spoke of a "a time to mourn and a time to dance"; there had been a lot of mourning in recent years but no dancing. As we rearranged our lives, a previously unknown door began to open, giving us a glimpse of a new season and resulting in three visits to Israel, with plenty of dancing! Each was a wonderful experience and would fill a whole book. I will focus on the first one, which came about almost by accident.

## ICEJ Tour

On Monday evenings, Dulcie hosted a prayer for Israel group at her home. She and Hugh were planning to lead a tour group to celebrate the Feast of Tabernacles in Israel, their third tour. Dulcie was struggling to manage the tour finances in a climate of constant bank rate fluctuation. My work experience was in finance, so I offered to help. Each Monday evening, I headed for her home immediately after work, and we would spend an hour before prayer group going through the payments received and calculating what each person still owed.

Miriam, the Israeli tour guide, invoiced the overall amount in US dollars required, which was then divided by the number of pilgrims. Accessing US dollars in Zimbabwe was challenging, and most pilgrims paid in instalments. A small deposit was required to secure the bookings, with full payment paid on arrival. Each pilgrim's payments were deposited into the tour's Forex Bank account. But as the bank rate changed, the amount mutated, and constant calculations were needed to determine how much each person had paid and what was owed.

What a headache! But it was during this exercise that the seeds were sown. A longing grew in both Brian and me to be part of the tour. As information was received from Miriam highlighting places to be visited, excitement bubbled. These places were familiar from reading the Bible, and now they became real. But we just did not have the funds to join the group, so this dream was put on the "back-burner". Maybe, next year we'd be in Jerusalem.

Then, out of the blue, Brian was offered a short-term contract in Nigeria with a British company, contouring farmland and teaching villagers. Payment would be in sterling—more than enough for the Israel trip! Had God opened the door? Made a way when there seemed no way? We had not prayed specifically to be part of the tour group, but God knew our hearts. Our Heavenly Father blessed us after the horror of Katie's sudden death the previous year.

A round trip was booked on El Al, the Israeli national carrier, including a UK visit with brothers and sisters, nieces and nephews, cousins, and friends. Brother Alan loaned us a car, and we travelled the length and breadth of the United Kingdom, spending time with family and making memories.

One event left us all shaken, when Brian was injured playing soccer with his nephews and nieces. He was taken to outpatients fearing a broken arm. But, Praise God, it was just a chipped elbow. His arm was strapped and placed in a sling with instructions given—"no lifting".

So, what about those suitcases? Enter the BSG (big strong girl).

## Heading to the Promised Land!

We turned our faces towards Israel on 13 October as brother Mike drove us to London for the night flight to Tel Aviv. The cross-examination at London Airport by Israeli security was a reminder that we were heading for a war zone. Passengers were almost all Israelis, returning to Israel to celebrate Sukkot, one of the three most important Feasts of the Lord.

We dozed through the night and were woken at dawn as the Jewish men moved to the back of the plane for morning prayers. This was our first experience of the sight and sounds of Jewish men at prayer—they rocked and sang, enclosed in a dazzling array of blue and white prayer shawls, their gold and silver threads catching the first rays of the sun.

As the plane circled Tel Aviv Airport, preparing to land, passengers and crew began to sing, "Yevanhu Shalom Alechem" (We come to bring you God's peace), clapping, rejoicing, and giving us goosebumps.

We disembarked to another sobering round of questioning and security checks, but joy welled up as we exited the airport building. We were standing on Israeli soil—ready to walk in the footsteps of Yeshua!

We trundled our luggage around the corner to the taxi rank. The taxi driver recognised the address and loaded up the suitcases, and we headed north and inland. When we arrived at Ramat Rachel, the driver pointed to the fare to be paid, and we added a tip, Zimbabwe style. Did we insult him? Or was the tip not enough? He was disgruntled as he dumped the suitcases on the pavement and sped away, leaving me to carry them into the hotel unaided, despite Brian's arm visibly in a sling.

A major revamp was underway at the impressive Ramat Rachel Hotel. But they were still receiving guests. The tariffs had been greatly reduced during the rebuild inconvenience, which allowed cash-strapped Zimbabweans to be guests for three nights at a potentially five-star establishment! The location was ideal, outside of the main city, on an elevated site overlooking the shepherds' field towards Bethlehem and on a regular bus route.

As we signed in, we heard a yoo-hoo from Jeni, our friend from Nyanga. She and John had arrived earlier from Canada, where they had been visiting one of their daughters. John was feeling unwell and resting. So, after depositing the luggage in our rooms, Jeni, Brian, and I headed to the bus stop for our first experience of Jerusalem, the city of the Great King.

### Firsts

There were so many *firsts* on this first of our three pilgrimages. We took the number 7 bus to Jaffa Road and walked through the Mahane Yehuda Market—my first real food market. It was crowded, with people loading their shopping baskets and shouting to each other amid the mounds of fruit, vegetables, and nuts. In our haste to see Jerusalem we had missed lunch, so were easily enticed by the aromas from a falafel vendor— another first for me.

That was when I discovered my purse was missing! Had I left it at the hotel or at the bus stop? Determined not to let anything dampen our enthusiasm, we prayed for its recovery and meandered through the streets outside the city walls, just revelling in sights and smells.

I was fascinated by the formally dressed Orthodox Jews and wanted to take a picture, but Jeni shook her head. Brian managed to capture one of me looking at a notice board just as the men happened to walk by. We gazed at the Montefiore Windmill and walked through the flashier suburb of King David, towards the Old City. The cream Jerusalem stone glowed gold with the sun's afternoon rays as we had our first sighting of the city walls. We just stood in awe, basking in the knowledge that Jesus could have walked here.

It was time to catch the bus back to Ramat Rachel. When we arrived at our stop, at the end of the line, there was my purse—on the seat, intact, just as I had left it, waiting for collection! Thank you Yeshua, for answered prayer.

The rest of the group had arrived and was being directed to rooms in the annexe, where we slept. That first night was an early night for everyone. Breakfast in the main dining room became our main meal of the day, with a roll and piece of fruit often stashed into handbags for lunch!

## The Old City

Next day, we were herded back into the city straight after breakfast under the guidance of our leader, Hugh! The Old City was entered at Jaffa Gate, the ancient streets already crowded with tourists visiting for Sukkot. Hugh led us firstly through the Christian sector, past several churches including the Church of the Holy Sepulchre and then onto the Via Dolorosa, the way of the Cross. As we meandered through narrow streets of the Jewish sector, the heavens opened with a deluge of rain, scattering the group to shelter in doorways.

When we regathered, Brian, Lovemore, and Edward were missing! After waiting for a few minutes, we decided to press on without them. But, as we walked through the streets, we passed a bookstore, and there were the boys.

Next stop was the Western Wall, where there were already crowds praying—men and women positioned along separate parts of the wall. We remained in the Western Wall plaza as a group, praying for the peace of Jerusalem. As we watched, rosy-cheeked 12-year-olds, yarmulkes slightly awry, were bar-mitzvahed by sombre rabbis in Hassidic dress. The swaying young men read their portion of the scriptures, their fathers by their side and their mothers hanging over the dividing wall. The celebrations were accompanied by singing and sometimes ended with dancing. This reminded us of Jesus remaining at the temple after his family had started their journey home. Was this Jesus's bar mitzvah?

From our vantage point in the plaza, we could see both mosques on Temple Mount, but access to the top of Mount Zion was guarded by Israeli soldiers. On a later trip Sally, Libby, and I were granted entry to the Mount after being told sternly, "No praying!" Yeah right!

We did not fall on our faces or rock back and forth but prayed for Yeshua's return as we paced—measuring the distance between the two mosques. Yes! There is space for the third temple.

The time between Tisha B'Av and Sukkot is when Zionists attempt to position an altar on the Mount, using helicopters, each carrying a section. This is seen as representing the third temple, heralding the coming of the Messiah. We were able to view the items assembled by the Temple Institute to be used in the third temple.

Our second day ended with a walk through the Arab quarter. It was filled with wonderfully colourful displays by shop owners, who called out to passing tourists, inviting them into their shops for coffee—and purchases. The number 7 bus was already filled with city workers and Yeshiva students when we headed back to Ramat Rachel.

## More Sightseeing

The following day was an official tour day. Driver Se'ev and tour guide David collected us after breakfast to drive us back to the Old City and further afield. We sang in St Anne's Church, a mediaeval Church with amazing acoustics, which served a season as a mosque. Many tears were shed at Yad Vashem; my own tears started to flow when viewing the of piles of suitcases preserved after their owners had been gassed. We stood in awe on the Mount of Olives overlooking the Golden Gate, firmly closed now, awaiting the arrival (Second Coming) of our Messiah. As one of the younger pilgrims said, "I know these places, I just haven't been here before."

The Garden of Gethsemane has large, ancient olive trees, with huge trunks, that would have been growing in Jesus's day! These trees split when they reach maximum height and weight, but the trees don't die; they coppice and grow again. Symbolic of Jesus's death and resurrection?

The Chagall windows at Hadassah Hospital were a highlight for me. And lunch at a café come gift shop owned by a family of Arab Christians, former residents of Bethlehem, gave us a glimpse of the conflict between Arabs and Jews. We learned how this family had been driven from Bethlehem, how'd they lost homes and business and had started again in Jerusalem. David and Se'ev shepherded us back to the hotel to process all we had experienced in one day.

## Erev Sukkot

Next morning, our bags were packed, and we left Ramat Rachel after breakfast. Today's sightseeing would take us up to Masada; most of the group took the funicular, but some of the hardy fellows felt the need to walk. Se'ev shared the history of this seemingly impregnable mountain, the place where David fled from Saul, where Herod the Great built two palaces, and where 960 Jewish zealots who opposed Roman occupation died, ending the first Jewish-Roman war in 74 CE.

Then we were driven down to the Dead Sea, where we bobbed in the salt lake, relaxing in the sun before heading up to Qumran. This is where the Dead Sea scrolls were found in jars stored in caves. And it was where the opening ICEJ celebration would take place on Erev Sukkot. We arrived around four thirty and parked among fleets of other tour busses. Some 4,000 Christians from all over the world gathered to share a meal and fellowship, the start the Feast of Tabernacle Celebration. Sukkot started at sundown with the blowing of the shofar, calling us to worship. And worship our Lord we did, under the stars! It was a wonderfully uplifting and joyful experience, setting the tone for the rest of the seven-day feast.

It was after midnight when we arrived at the small B and B hotel, which was to be our base for the next week, within easy walking distance of the conference centre. The days started early with prayers before breakfast and then the morning sessions at the feast—a choice of topics and speakers for each time slot. And a celebration each evening.

## Celebrating Yeshua Hamashiach

The First night of the ICEJ celebration was an assault on my senses! Musicians from around the world gathered into one orchestra—accompanying the choir and dancers. The 4,000 pilgrims from eighty nations, each in their national dress, packed the auditorium of the international conference centre. Candles were lit by representatives of each nation, and opening night speeches were given by leading Christian teachers and Israeli political leaders. I loved every moment. In fact, I loved every moment of the entire conference—the teaching, the celebration worship each evening; interaction with Christians from other countries in group activities, and mingling with Israelis and tourists on the Jerusalem March.

One evening as we walked to the evening celebration, a man dressed in Hasidic garb walked alongside Deidre addressing her quietly. She dropped back from the group and moved off the footpath, speaking intently to the man. The group stopped, watching and waiting for her to join us, but she swung her head towards the conference centre, giving us the carry-on-without-me sign.

We walked on, waiting a little anxiously around the corner. Some Jerusalem Jews were resentful of the hordes of Christians taking over their city, and we hoped Deidre was not in danger. Later we heard that the man had singled her out as someone who looked Jewish, her colouring and mode of dress, and wanted to ask questions. He was reading the New Testament and learning about Yeshua, discovering Jesus was a Jew not a Gentile. Was he the promised Messiah? Deidre was the perfect choice to answer his questions! This was my first glimpse, in 1997, of the gospel reaching the people who first received it from Yeshua in AD 30.

## Galilee

The final night was a joyous celebration with dancing in the aisles, music, and singing that continued until midnight. The following morning, we bade farewell to the City of Kings, rejoining our tour guides to travel north. The first stop was Yardenit baptismal site, where nine or ten candidates from our group were baptised, either first baptisms or recommitments. Brian and I had both received baptism by total emersion so did not go into the Jordan River on that trip. In 2001, when we were leading the tour, Brian was the one in the water baptising, and I was baptised by my husband—a rededication of both our marriage and our walk with Jesus.

Next stop was Tiberias, where we boarded a boat, similar in size and shape to the fishing boats of Jesus's day. We sailed across the Sea of Galilee to Ein Gev, where we were served a lunch described as "Saint Peter's fish". Then back to Tiberias and on to Capernaum. This was another highlight for me. Standing in the ruins of the synagogue where Jesus preached, reading the words he had spoken, brought the gospel to life!

Back in the bus, we headed towards Dor visiting en route, the worship centre being constructed on Mount Carmel. That elevated place, where Isaiah had called down the fire of the Lord, provided a panoramic view of the Valley of Megiddo, and much discussion of the final war in Revelation.

Two nights at a Moshav in Dor and a swim in the Mediterranean Sea put us in holiday relaxing mode, allowing us time to process our experiences before the heading back to Tel Aviv for the flight to Zimbabwe.

## Renewed Faith

Returning home after those weeks in Israel was really coming down to earth from the mountaintop! But we returned with a deeper understanding of our faith and made changes in the way we worshipped. We began to intentionally keep the Sabbath. Each Friday night, a group of us would meet for prayer, and a Shabbat meal. Brian learned the She'ma, both spoken and sung, and printed the dialogue and responses in Hebrew for us to take part in Shabbat prayers. In 1998, a Passover celebration was held in our garden attended by about thirty people sharing a traditional Passover meal, followed by dancing led by Barbara and her group. All were members of ICEJ, from a mix of churches, regularly praying for the peace of Israel.

Doors opened for two more visits to the Holy Land—each one revealing more about our Jewish roots and deepening our relationship with Yeshua HaMashiach. The plans for a fourth - tour were scuttled by more political upheaval.

# TWENTY-FIVE

# A Time to Scatter

**2000, Millennium: Regathering**

The year of 1999 was one of re-gathering. Nick and Ann returned to Zimbabwe in time for Jonathan's third birthday, Ann pregnant with Meghan. As the year drew to a close, there was speculation and anxiety about the turn of the century. Would computer systems crash when 2000 rolled up, taking all telecommunication down with them? Craig, Karen, and Ben travelled to Zimbabwe from New Zealand to celebrate the millennium with us.

On New Year's Eve, we all boarded the houseboat *Shambira*, planning to see in the new century from Lake Kariba. Nick needed to be close to the shore, for his work, just in case everything shut down at midnight, so the houseboat was moored off Antelope Island. We bedded down on the top deck under the stars, with a panoramic view of the fireworks on the mainland. The joyous sounds of celebration mingled with the grunts of hippos and splashes of crocodiles.

*Marie Bishop*

## Rustle in the Wind

In April 2000, those infamous "winds of change" began to rustle in our own lives. Ann, Nick, and children joined Brian and me on holiday in Natal. We spent two weeks of coastal bliss in beautifully appointed three-bedroomed holiday accommodation, with panoramic views of the Indian Ocean. The apartment block was surrounded by tropical trees shading a lawn, with a pathway leading onto the beach. Mornings were spent swimming and building sandcastles with Jono, followed by after-lunch naps. As we dozed, the monkeys in the trees watched for the right moment to leap over the balustrade, scoot across the lounge, grab bananas from the fruit bowl, and dash back to the tree, under the astonished gaze of dozy adults!

On one restful afternoon, I glanced over at Nicholas, stretched out in a chair and reading a book, which he was holding at face height. Why was he covering his face? Had he been at the biscuit tin or sneaking an ice cream? No! He wanted me to see the title of the book he was reading! *How to Immigrate to Australia*.

What?! I reached across and pulled the book from his face. "What are you telling me?" I asked.

He laughed, a bit sheepishly I later realised, claiming, "Just an interesting read, Ma."

The interest in reading about Australia could have been fuelled by the shocking news report we'd watched on TV earlier that week. David Stevens, a farmer in Zimbabwe, had been murdered and his farm taken. Five other farmers who had come to David Steven's aid were abducted, beaten, and later released with injuries requiring hospitalisation. We were in shock but also in disbelief. Surely this was an isolated incident. But no, David Stevens was the first of many.

"The Fast Track Land Reform" had begun (*The Guardian*, 17 April 2000).

As security deteriorated in Zimbabwe, the Telco Nick worked for explored new ventures in other countries. He was offered the opportunity to move to Swaziland or New Zealand, creating new networks. New Zealand became his immigration country of choice, as there was already a family network—Craig, Karen, and Ben, plus newer immigrants Nick's uncle, aunt, and cousins.

We had fallen into a pattern of Sunday catch-ups; Ann and Nick attended church in Greystone Park so would usually come for lunch after their service. One such Sunday, Henry Olonga was a visiting speaker at their church GP, finishing his talk by singing "My Zimbabwe", which impacted most of the congregation. This was the day Ann and Nick planned to tell Brian and me that their plan to emigrate to New Zealand in January was underway. By the time Ann reached our house, she was a basket case, sobbing, her face streaked with tears.

"You will come!" she begged. The most we could promise was a holiday visit when they were settled. Few countries welcomed immigrants in their sixties, unless there was wealth accompanying them. My pension was non-remittable. Brian's business would sustain us in our senior years, but we were not wealthy so could not see emigration as an option.

## Letting Go, Again

Ann, Nick, and the children moved in with us, as their home was packed up, and we had four weeks to enjoy them before they flew away, to the ends of the earth! There were lots of last-time outings, to favourite places with favourite friends. Christmas Day lunch at our home, where Ann had lived since she was 4, was bittersweet for Brian and me. Would this be our last family Christmas?

On departure day, I was determined not to weep and wail—to focus on keeping calm, especially for Ann. There were plenty of tears shed as friends came to the airport for final farewells. I held it together until they went through to the departure lounge, and then the wheels came off! When would we ever see them again? They had been a big part of our lives, sharing Jonathan and Meghan from the day each one was born. Life without them was unimaginable, unbearable.

This was my retirement year too, after twenty years with the company! The days emptied with no work, no family, and too much time on my hands. But not for long!

A small accounting business began to evolve when Pastor John Chinyamba asked me to take over the accounts for a charity he ran. I was already "doing the books" for Brian's business, and our church plant so this made three sets of books. It was time to make this more efficient. I registered for a course and installed a computer programme to cope with multiple small businesses.

## Brian's Timbers Business

Brian's business was operating at capacity for the size of the small industrial site. He had three portable sawmills, one fuelled by petrol, one by diesel, and a fixture at the workshop, converted to electrical power. Trees were felled and milled into timber on site using either the diesel or petrol mill, depending on whichever fuel was available during times of shortage due to Zimbabwe's financial crisis. If no petrol or diesel could be had, the logs were ferried back to the workshop in Brian's custom-made trailer and converted into building-sized timber using the electric powered mill. Three milling options kept the business going. The staff of eight trained men left their homes in the dawn light to be at the collection point by 7.30 a.m., often walking if there were no busses.

My contribution was sourcing bread to provide a simple breakfast before the men started their day. Most days started with a bakery crawl to all the local bakeries and supermarkets. There were times when none was available, and I was offered flour to bake my own! The men were very generous with their thanks, but I know my bread-making skills were almost non-existent. Loading it with jam made it palatable.

## Shake-up

During 2002, amid reports of white-owned small businesses being targeted and closed, BB Timbers came under scrutiny from the Ministry of Labour. I was at home when Brian called, asking me to bring the books, all of them, into the workshop. Two solemn, unsmiling men were waiting when I arrived. Both were large, filling the tiny office space. One towered over me and ignored my outstretched hand. I deposited the ledgers on the desk and backed out to make them cups of tea. For the next hour, they studied the figures and conferred over entries. They were particularly absorbed in the information regarding staff salaries, holiday allowance, sick leave, and loans—and one item they had never seen before!

"What does this mean?!" asked the very large man. He was pointing to an entry on the loans page: "Cancelled. Jubilee year!"

Where was Brian? How was I going to explain the principle of jubilee?

All of the employees needed loans at times, but one

member of staff regularly borrowed more than he could pay back. His finances were always a mess. In Leviticus 25, God commanded that, every fiftieth year, the year following seven times seven, all debts were to be wiped and a new start made. Brian had decided at the start of 2002 to apply the Old Testament principle of Jubilee and guide the men on budgeting, especially Isaac. Now I could only try to explain this concept.

"My husband decided to cancel all the debts owed by the staff and start the new year with a clean slate," I said. "This is a biblical principal."

The men from the ministry looked puzzled. "So, when do they need to pay the loans back?" the thinner one asked.

"Never," I answered. "The debt is cancelled. There is one other thing, though. There will be no more loans. If money is needed, it will be an advance of salary. This way, there should be no unmanageable debt building up."

The two men stared at me without understanding and then turned back to the ledgers. I took the opportunity to move outside and do a stock count, while they spoke with some of the men in the workshop. Shortly they came into the timber yard.

"We are finished now, madam." Both extended their hands.

"Is everything okay?" I asked.

"Oh yes! Everything is very good," the larger man said, smiling as he waved to the staff and headed for the gate.

Phew! Brian and I were relieved. We had been given the ministry approval.

But that experience had shaken us. And then another incident came two weeks later—a burglary! Locks were broken and machinery stolen over a weekend. The police were onto it rapidly and soon tracked down the burglar, Brian's foreman,

Danford, the first man Brian had employed. He had absolutely no skills but was desperate for work and a family to care for. Brian had trained him and promoted him to foreman in charge of the workshop staff, with a good salary, but it was obviously not enough.

The full story emerged. It was Danford who had called in the Ministry of Labour on trumped-up charges of underpaying staff. When the business was not closed down by the ministry, he stole machinery, intending to set up in opposition. The machinery was recovered, and the police were persuaded not to press charges; dismissal and loss of income would be hard enough on Danford's wife and four children.

## Con Man

Flights had been booked to visit to New Zealand in June, but we were shocked when our friend and travel agent, Brenda, told us the fare had to be paid in Rand not Zim dollars! The bank turned down our request for forex. Holiday travel was not a priority in a country with a declining economy. It seemed Rand could only be bought on the black market.

Our young neighbour worked at a large city hotel and offered to source Rand for us, but the exchange rate would be high! I phoned Brian to tell him the dollars needed. "That is a rip-off," he said. "We need to keep looking. Surely we can get the money at a better rate than that!"

One of his customers, overhearing his side of the conversation, offered a lower rate through his nephew and arranged for us to meet on Saturday to make the exchange.

Cash was withdrawn from our savings account, and we arrived at the appointed place, an inconspicuous parking under a tree in the Avenues. A young man approached the car. "Mr Bishop?" he asked.

He got into the back of our car, shaking hands with Brian and me. "I am Tendayi, I have the R2,000 my uncle said you needed," he said, brandishing a bulging envelope. "Do you have the dollars?"

We exchanged envelopes and each counted the contents. He returned the Zim dollar envelope to us with a down-turned mouth and held out his hand for the Rands to be returned.

"I was expecting more than this," he said.

"That is the amount your uncle asked for," Brian replied "We don't have any more cash with us. That's the rate we agreed on."

Silence while he thought about it. Then, pointing across the road, he called, "Quick! look over there! A policeman."

My heart started to beat furiously as I saw a policeman standing on the corner, looking in our direction. We knew we were breaking the law but had accepted this was the way money changed hands under rigid exchange regulations. Tendayi thrust the envelope into Brian's hand while grabbing our dollars from mine. He jumped out of the car saying, "Go quickly!"

We did. Brian put his foot on the accelerator, and we sped around the corner, leaving the policeman standing. Phew!

I opened the envelope to count the Rand, and my heart sank. R10 notes were top and bottom of the stack but between them was a pile of useless ZW$5 notes! We had been conned. What fools we had been! What utter, greedy, faithless fools!

My trip was off. Our savings were gone. I felt bleak and so ashamed. We had followed the way of the world in sourcing finance, instead of taking our request to our loving Heavenly Father, who owns the cattle on a thousand hills! I sank down to my knees to confess my sin to the Lord—realising I should have been on my knees before the transaction.

My bible fell open at Jeremiah 10:17 (NIV): "Gather up your belongings to leave the land." Was God telling us it was time to leave Zimbabwe? We had been asking that question for a while. Another reason for my trip was to check if we could transplant to New Zealand, a sort of reconnaissance.

Now that opportunity was lost.

# TWENTY-SIX

# A Time for Reconnaissance

Brian called a day of prayer and fasting on 1 May, May Day! It was a call for help and also a national holiday in Zimbabwe, Workers' Day.

Our confidence was really shaken by recent events. We felt vulnerable. Who could we trust going forward? What would our long- term future be?

We were up early to start the day of prayer, each heading to a different part of the garden with our Bibles, no breakfast or even morning tea until we sought the Lord and heard from Him what His will for us was. I took a folding chair to a private spot by the stream under the willow trees. Brian stayed closer to the house under the Jacaranda tree.

So how did I do this? How would I hear God's voice? And how would I know it was God speaking and not just my thoughts?

I opened my Bible and read the WFT passage for today. It came from Mark 7:21(NIV) and read, "For from within, out of men's hearts come evil thoughts, sexual immorality, theft."

Was God confirming that the con man, Tendayi, was a thief? He had stolen our savings.

"Punish him Lord, please," I called out.

I continued reading. "Murder, adultery, greed." Had it been our greed that had caused us to reject a more secure exchange offer? Had God arranged this reliable source of funding? I prayed then to repent of my greed and the sin of breaking the law.

And I continued to read. "Malice, deceit, lewdness, envy, slander, arrogance, and folly!" *Folly*! I had no idea folly was a sin that would make me unclean. I had already acknowledged what fools we were, and now I confessed it as sin, begging God's forgiveness. I also knew He was telling me to forgive Tendayi. That was not going to be easy. I had screamed abuse down the phone when Brian called his customer, Tendayi's uncle. Now God was telling me I needed to forgive. I spoke words of forgiveness but knew this was something I would really need to work at.

I sat quietly, wondering what next. Was that it? The sun was casting rays of light around me. Weaver birds were flitting to and from their nests hanging from the willow trees. I could hear their twittering, but no voice from heaven. Then into my mind dropped Micah 2. I felt as though it had been written on my forehead!

I opened my NIV Bible to Micah 2. Which verse? Where to start? I started from the beginning. "Woe to those who plan iniquity, to those who plot evil on their beds! At morning's light they carry it out because it is in their power to do it. They covet fields and seize them, and houses and take them. They defraud a man of his home, a fellowman of his inheritance" (Micha 2:1–2).

This was happening in Zimbabwe. Fields (farms) had been seized, former productive land lying fallow, causing food

213

shortages bordering on famine. Would homes become targets? Would the Ministry of Housing be visiting us next on the heels of the Ministry of Labour? My heart sank.

I continued reading. Verse 3 said, "I am planning disaster against this people, from which you cannot save yourselves." The *you* leapt out at me! Were these words for Brian and me? We would be especially vulnerable, no family to turn to with all of them having left or leaving Zimbabwe. Fay and Bill were planning to move to England next year, and my cousins, Arlene and Bob were counting down, too. We would be entirely without family support.

I needed to speak to Brian. Would he accept this scripture as God's warning, in answer to our prayers? I headed back to the house.

As I approached, the smell of bacon frying filled the air. Brian was whistling at the stove as he pushed the sizzling bacon round the pan. "Tea's made" he said.

"Did God speak to you?" I asked.

"Did He give you an answer?"

"Sure did," he said, smiling. "In Micah 2."

"What?! That's the same reading He gave me!" I read him the first three verses, which God gave me.

"Mine was different," he said. "I just prayed, opened my Bible at random, and my eyes hit on Micah 2:10. 'Get up, go away, for this is not your resting place because it is defiled, it is ruined.' That couldn't be clearer," said Brian.

Typical! Just ask God, get the answer, go inside, and make the tea. No second-guessing. We ate our breakfast out on the veranda, gazing onto the lovely garden surrounding this home that he had built. The realisation that we would be leaving it all behind, hit me, with tears.

"God didn't say where to go to, just to go!" Brian said

thoughtfully. "We can always go back to our roots in England if we can't go to New Zealand. God will open the right doors."

And He did.

## Abundant Blessing

Our phone rang at lunchtime next day, Jean calling from Johannesburg. Dee had told her all the sordid details of the con. They were in South Africa to sort out Jean's inheritance from her godmother and, hopefully, buy a holiday home with the proceeds.

"Now listen, Marie," she said, "phone the agent and rebook that flight. Brian and I wanted to tithe on my aunt's money, and we have deposited R2000 in your Building Society account. No buts. You need to go!"

I was speechless—overcome! What a gift from my wonderful friends. Jean has been a blessing to me in so many ways, I could only thank the Lord for what she had done. I'm not sure if that is the scriptural way to tithe, but it certainly ticked the WWJD box!

My trip was on again. I could gather my belongings to leave the land! We would first check out if New Zealand, not England was to be our new home.

## Family Down Under

Ann and Nick were settling into their Kiwi home in Sunnynook. We communicated regularly by phone and emails, following their progress. They were still looking for a new church home, attending services at churches in the area. Ann and Meghan attended Mainly Music at one of the local Churches, a fun activity for Mums and toddlers. Jonathan started his school life at a local Christian school. just a short drive from their home, with friendly staff teaching and caring for 500 pupils.

Jonathan had always been a sunny, smiley boy, chuckling at an early age! But now, he was living in a strange land, a new boy at school who spoke differently to the other children, and he was not so smiley. Every person in his young life, apart from his immediate family, had disappeared. His teacher was originally from Bulawayo. She understood what he had lost and prayed and guided him through this traumatic time as he struggled with the change. Ann pointed out cars like Nana's car and Grandpa's truck to maintain continuity. A visit from Nana would let him know his grandparents were still part of his life.

## Thirty-Five Hours of Travel

Brenda arranged flights with Singapore Airways, the cheapest but also the longest—ten hours from Johannesburg to Singapore, another ten hours flying to Auckland, with a fifteen-hour stopover in Singapore! A daybed would have cost US$200, a huge amount at the inflated Zim dollar exchange rate. I resolved to push through, sleep on each flight, and survive the fifteen hours somehow.

But those hours turned into a memorable day! Firstly, a free tour was offered by the airline—a busload of sojourners visiting the sights of this wonderful city, including beaches and the zoo. Upon return to the airport, after a meal courtesy of the airline, I found a quiet corner to stretch out. My handbag was tucked under me, coat over me, and I slept for an hour. Refreshed, I walked around the terminal building and stumbled on a quiz show, the host encouraging bystanders to take part. Hesitant at first, I took a place. The audience were all strangers. I knew not a soul, so no one cared about my stupid answers! And I thoroughly enjoyed the experience. Needless to say, I did not win the prize! But it proved to be a very pleasant interlude.

## Family Reunion

The family were all at the airport to meet me with hugs and lots of laughter. They had planned good use of my six weeks, showcasing what New Zealand had to offer. Craig, Karen, and Ben headed back to Hawkes Bay, leaving me to be spend the first 2 weeks in Auckland. Sharing everyday life gave me a sense of how normal life would be. There'd be none of the tensions and challenges experienced in Zimbabwe—replaced instead by shopping with Ann and Meghan in the mornings and collecting Jono from school and heading for the beach, building sandcastles, even in winter! Their friends welcomed me too. It was great to put faces to names and to attend "their" new church.

Nick had taken a few days leave to have a trip around the Waikato. Craig, Karen, and Ben met us at Rotorua, where we all stayed at a holiday park. The sights and smells, the volcanic activity, the Maori village at Whakawerawera, gave a glimpse into a whole new world. We drove around the Blue and Green Lakes, Rainbow Springs, the Agrodome and relaxed in the Polynesian Spa. Nick, Ann, and children headed back to Auckland, while I travelled with the Hawkes Bay family to their new home.

Hawkes Bay had a totally different vibe. We travelled over the mountains coming into a flatter agricultural area, with splashy flower farms and hectares of grapes to fuel the many wineries. The Hawkes Bay Bishops were living in Te Awanga, with the pebbled beach at the end of their garden. I was able to see Ben's school, and Craig's work and enjoyed spas with Karen and a glass of wine after walks on the beach. There were visits to the gannet colony and Art Deco Napier; shopping in the local village; and, of course, tastings at wineries and a special farewell meal.

The trip back to Auckland for my final week was by bus, affording an almost bird's-eye views of the countryside. Those weeks confirmed to me that New Zealand should be our destination—not the United Kingdom. I loved everything about New Zealand, especially having all my family in one country.

Walking through that door would take a little longer than we expected.

Christ church Home Group

Katie

Katie

Brian and Ben

Bishop Family – Ann and Nick' wedding

Read Family – Ann and Nick's wedding

Craig and Karen's wedding

# WINTER

# TWENTY-SEVEN

# A Time to Pull up Roots

## Releasing the Ties

One of Brian's fears was the New Zealand winters, remembering his childhood. Visiting in winter allowed me to report back that we could handle the lower temperatures. Nothing like the British winters I assured him, especially in the North Island. "It doesn't even snow in Auckland!"

God had told us to move, had instructed us to leave Zimbabwe. "Get up and go away, for this is not your resting place." But He had not told us the destination. My holiday had confirmed that New Zealand was the place for us. It made sense to be in the same country as Craig, Ann, and all our grandchildren. Also, it was in my DNA, as Grandpa Parker was a Kiwi. So, it was agreed we would uproot and move to the other side of the world. But, the actual uprooting took another year.

Brian wanted to sell his business as a going concern, keeping the staff employed. He started the process of advertising and interviewing This was a great wrench for him, having built the business up from scratch. Would this be his last venture? Could we start another business in New Zealand? The possibility was discussed—maybe another shop? We would need to work for at least ten years before qualifying for New Zealand superannuation. At ages 64 and 68, when most people are retiring, we really were starting again!

There were also decisions to be made about the house, whether to sell or rent. Capital was non-remittable from Zimbabwe and subject to hefty capital gains taxes, so we decided to rent and not sell. Hopefully, one fine day, the Zimbabwean economy would revive, and we could look forward to realising our investment. Our friends Ian and Christine offered to be the house agents, overseeing the property and rent payment, for a small commission. This was an answer to prayer.

We knew we would need to be "wise as serpents and cunning as foxes" to make this move and avoid becoming a burden on our children. The Zimbabwe Reserve Bank froze all bank accounts when emigration applications were received, so we decided to apply for retirement holiday visas. This came with the added bonus of a once-in-a-lifetime holiday allowance! Once this was confirmed, an application was made directly to the reserve bank requesting release of funds to ship some furniture and precious items to our children in New Zealand. The reason given was that we were downsizing, and this was their inheritance. Absolutely true; we just omitted to say we were downsizing in New Zealand. Our application was granted. A container was loaded with furniture, Brian's tools, and even a new electric lawn mower and taken away for storage until shipping could be arranged.

Forms were submitted to the New Zealand embassy requesting holiday visas; these were usually granted for three to six months, but ours came back as one-year visas! We could apply for residency, allowing us to work once we were in New

Zealand, but until then our retirement holiday allowances would be our means of support.

Then another miracle came. When shares jointly in the names of Brian and Craig were sold, the full return from these was remitted to Craig's Australian account, where we could access the funds. God was paving the way!

## New Home for the Sabaos

Tenants were found for our house, a young family needing a new start after a hard year. They agreed to keep Gabriel working for them but were reluctant to have Loveness and the three children living in the staff cottage. Provision for these faithful employees/friends had been high on our agenda. But we had seen our own pensions shrink so could not rely on providing a monthly pension for the Sabao family.

We decided to build them a home of their own before we left. Gabriel was originally from Mozambique, not Zimbabwe born so not entitled to rural tribal land, and their earned income would not be enough to cover rates and services in the urban areas. Brian applied to Chief Chinamora for land in Domboshawa, and we were interviewed by two of his sons. (Rumour had it that there were 100 children!) They agreed to sell us a piece of land in a newly developed section. Currently, there were no services, but electricity for the area was at planning stage, as there was a new high school opening shortly, within walking distance for their son, Blessing.

We all went on a reconnaissance trip! The section bordered on a game park with deer wandering by the east side of the high fence. Lovely kopjes bordered the west side, and it was a big piece of land—plenty of space for chickens and vegetables. It was an ideal spot. Gabriel signed on the dotted line; Brian paid the chiefs and building started. It was a small cottage—living room, kitchen, bathroom, and two bedrooms, with a veranda to watch the sunset. A well was dug hitting a high water table providing good supply and a hand pump installed "kaminakawena" style. The Sabao family had a home!

Brian's timber business was sold—heart-wrenching for him to walk away from his dream after having built it from the ground up. The new owner retained the staff, a major concern, but it was an emotional day when Brian handed over the keys to the workshop and the truck.

## Leaving

We prepared ourselves to head for pastures new. Departure day was pushed back to the end of August, due to delayed Australian travel visas. We were disappointed not to be there for Jonathan's birthday and Bethany's birth. But this meant we could attend the wedding of our friends, Kate and Nico, a wonderful celebration. But also bittersweet, as we said goodbye to so many people who had shared our lives. Sally gave us beds for the last two nights; our last supper was at a Borrowdale restaurant with Sally, Fay, and Bill. And we boarded a plane for Johannesburg. God has blessed us with such wonderful, loving friends; it was so painful taking leave of them all! Would we ever see them again? I thought I had handled it all very well, until I saw the photographs later. My eyes were little red dots, sunk into a puffy face, swollen from weeping. The uprooting had taken its toll.

The days in Johannesburg were a breather between the stress of packing up to leave and starting the next chapter. There were still more heart-wrenching farewells to be made. John and Hazel, friends of fifteen years, were now living in

Johannesburg, close to their son and family. We had studied and prayed in the same home group and shared Nyanga holidays and many of life's ups and downs. It was hard to say good-bye to them and to our friends Denise and Hugh, who had been part of our lives for thirty years—since our girls were six years old! Every holiday in South Africa had included time spent with them—sometimes the entire holiday but at least a kick-start weekend.

We shared meals at restaurants and shopped as we always had, putting departure time on the back-burner until it was time to go. More weeping. Would my face ever recover? We smiled and hugged and said with assurance, "We will see you again"; but in truth we doubted this would ever happen.

We left Johannesburg on the afternoon of 24 August, arriving at Perth early the following morning. Then it was on to Melbourne and, finally, Sydney, where we waited for our connection to New Zealand—emotionally drained!

Our flight arrived at Auckland Airport shortly before midnight, twenty minutes early. We felt numbed after travelling for the best part of thirty hours. Airport lights dimmed as the last passengers were processed, and we sat on the benches surrounded by luggage, waiting for Nick to collect us.

But it wasn't just Nick; the whole family came running through the doors to greet us. Ann carried a piccolo with ten-day old Bethany. Jono and Meghan were in their PJs. Tears of joy and of relief were shed. Nick loaded the luggage into the two cars—the children dozing during the fifty-minute drive to Greenhithe.

Our new lives were about to begin.

# TWENTY-EIGHT

# A Time to Transplant

**New after New**

We fell into bed and slept until a thunderous sound woke us around 4 a.m. Was it an earthquake? The sight from our bedroom window was unbelievable. Two heavy-duty trucks rumbled by, each transporting half of a house! Were our tired eyes deceiving us? But no—in earthquake-prone New Zealand, homes are built of timber, not the brick and tile of Zimbabwe. Houses can be uplifted and moved from one site to another—moving at night to avoid traffic congestion. Here was our first "first!"

Around 7 a.m., as the sky lightened, Jonathan and Meghan crept into our bed, followed by baby Bethany, delivered with mugs of tea! Our first day in New Zealand started cuddled up to our grandchildren. Nick took Jono to school and Meg to kindy, leaving us to doze on and off—jet lag style. The jet lag of a thirty-two-hour journey, added to the ordeal of uprooting, had left us both disorientated.

Those first days were a blur, Nick and Ann wisely kept them low key until we found our feet. We met their close friends, Paula, Jim, and baby Lauren and visited local shops and beaches, gradually emerging from the fog to begin adjusting to a different way of life.

Craig, Karen, and Ben arrived from Hawkes Bay on Friday—all the family together reminded us why we had initiated this trauma. Karen's car had been upgraded, so they drove in two cars, bringing her "old" Bluebird for our use. This gave us a measure of independence, and Brian eagerly explored the new suburbs. It was months before I had the confidence to get behind the wheel, only after Ann coerced me into collecting the children from school! I was intimidated by the fast-moving traffic, and "new" road rules. But she insisted. "Mum, remember you were once an accounts executive. You can do this!"

On Sundays, we accompanied the family to their new church. My plan had been to move away from our Anglican roots in our new country and seize the opportunity to find a more evangelical fellowship. Ann and Nick's new church was a large congregation, with good teaching and vibrant worship—loud and noisy (according to Brian!).

Maybe we would need to keep looking.

## Hiccough

As we prepared to submit our papers and apply for permanent residency, we hit the first snag. This was a time factor. Craig, as a Kiwi citizen, was to be our sponsor for two years. But the law required him to have been living and working in New Zealand for three full years prior to sponsoring new immigrants. The three years since their return from Australia would be complete on 15 November, so we would need to hold onto our forms until then. Ann suggested we view these two plus months as a readjustment holiday.

On Monday, 17 November, we headed for the city, forms in hand, and hit another snag. The Department of Immigration was overwhelmed with applications and announced no more forms would be accepted until February 2004. This had a knock-on effect, as our medical examinations and police clearances would be out of date by February. We joined a queue to speak with an immigration official. He was empathetic and stamped the police clearance as accepted, but, the medicals would need to be redone before we could submit our forms in February.

This hiccough meant a further three months before we could find work and rent our own home. We drove down to Hawkes Bay to share the bad news with Craig and Karen and give Ann and Nick a break. My own spirits dropped during this time, and I became anxious. The "what ifs" and genuine fears kept me awake at night—shrinking bank balance, no work.

After a sleepless night in December I fell to my knees crying out to God. He led me to Psalm 61:2 (TLB): "Wherever I am, though far away at the ends of the earth ..." Yes, Lord! That's where I am—the ends of the earth! Then, the promise in verse 6 leapt out: "Added years of life as rich and full as those of many generations." I highlighted these verses in my Living Bible and would reread and stand on them whenever doubts crept in.

## New Church Home

Top of our to-do list was to find a church family. We had attended local churches, including Anglican St Michael's, a friendly and welcoming small congregation close to home. Brian felt comfortable with the familiar form of worship, so we became part of their congregation. Then, in October, a bright orange postcard arrived in the letter box, announcing the start of a new church in the suburb. Shore Grace Wesleyan Church would hold its first service in the Greenhithe Village Hall on 23 November.

"This is the one," I told Brian. "I just feel this will be our church."

The services were evening services, starting with a BBQ—even better! We could still go to St Michael's in the morning and then Shore Grace in the evening. The date was marked on the calendar. We were in Te Awanga on 23 November so missed the opening service but were there on 30 November and have been ever since. Our first Christmas in New Zealand was different to those in Africa. The pohutakawa trees blossomed along the beaches with bright red flowers, Kiwi Christmas trees! But the flowers used for church Christmas decorations were blue and white, not the red, white, and yellow used in Africa—different flowers in season. The weather was still cool enough for hot roast daytime meal, although summer was pushing through. Houses were decorated on the outside, and we were able to drive around suburbs to "see the lights".

## Legal residents

In February, we completed new medical examinations, submitted our immigration forms, and breathed sighs of relief when these were accepted. An agent was appointed; we were interviewed and monitored; and we finally received residency in April. My daughter remarked recently that it was a miracle there were no harsh words during those seven months of shared living. Ann and Nick truly were saints! Now, at last we could get out of their hair and make a new home.

The Manse at St Michael's Church was not being used by the current priest, and suitable tenants had not been found.

We were accepted as suitable, non-smokers with no pets. Our container had arrived, and we were soon unpacking boxes in our new home, a Lockwood in the heart of the village.

The large garage was ideal for Brian's workshop, where he manufactured wooden items, which were displayed and sold at Craftworld.

My application to be a carer at a rest home was accepted—a complete change after many years in finance. The work was hard but very rewarding and gave me a toe in the employment door and confidence to work in a new environment.

Later that year, I applied for a temporary credit control position. The interviewer "just happened to be" from Harare. Her parents lived in Greystone Park. She hired me with only a glance at my CV! Our Kiwi lives were taking shape.

## Emmaus

Another pivotal event which helped my roots go deeper was the Walk to Emmaus. Several of our new church friends had done the three-day retreat and shared the spiritual value of this. My new friend Raewyn invited and sponsored me for ladies walk number 34. This was not like other retreats I had attended. It was much more than prayer and Bible reading! The focus was allowing Jesus to be central in every part of our lives—dying to self while identifying and developing gifts to serve in our churches. Pilgrims came from all over New Zealand, each sponsored by someone who had done the retreat. Links were formed with individuals and churches.

There were about forty ladies on walk number 34. Testimonies and talks were given by members of the team, and then we divided into small table groups for discussion and often a fun activity too. As the three-day retreat ended, we were released to our fourth day, which is the rest of our lives, and were encouraged to meet regularly with other pilgrims.

I was invited to join an existing fourth day group, which had been together for several years. The dynamic has changed over time as members moved off shore, but we support each other in prayer. Five of us continue to meet on Thursday evenings, sharing moments in our faith journeys and enjoying meals.

## Becoming Kiwis

When our three years on residents visas were completed, we applied for New Zealand citizenship. A date was set for the ceremony, giving us a new identity. After being a liver bird in my youth, a Zimbabwe bird for most of my adult years, now I would become a Kiwi! Our Zimbabwe passports had expired shortly after arrival; the renewal process from a distance was viewed as both problematic and costly. We had been grounded for those three years but now could apply for Kiwi passports and plan holidays. We could explore the islands or visit friends in Australia.

Top on our list was investing in a new home. We had skirted around the Zimbabwe capital gains law by selling number 8 to an offshore buyer but for well below value, giving us only a small capital to work with. Weekends were spent viewing potential houses for sale, but those in our price range were disappointing—depressing even.

Nick suggested that we build a "minor dwelling" on the unused portion of their land. His neighbours agreed to sell a small piece of their land to allow entrance from the next road, and Brian began drawing up plans. A two-bedroomed cottage with a garage/workshop below emerged on paper.

The future was looking rosy!

# TWENTY-NINE

# A Time to Mourn
# Brian, 1936–2007

**Goals in Brian's Diary**

The year, 2007, started out with so much hope! Christmas and New Year were spent at Te Awanga, a memory making family time. Brian recorded his goals for the coming year—building the cottage was top of the list, a minor dwelling for the majors. Another item on Brian's list was to have his moles checked.

Brian's diary entries always made good reading; he kept a record of happenings in the family, as well as newspaper cuttings of important events—important to him that is. So, if anyone wants to know about an earth tremor or when we had a family outing, Brian's diary is the place to look. He also kept a record of the current petrol prices.

Here are a few entries:

- 8 January: Visit to skin cancer clinic—biopsy of two squamous cancer moles and an all over scan. Mind set

at rest about mole; it is an "old-age spot". So, it seems I will live a while longer! Petrol $1.429 per litre.
- 9 January: Flame lilies start blooming, visit from our friends the Blackwells"

(These were normal events—no hint that our lives were about to change forever.)

- 10 January: Saw Dr J again at skin cancer clinic— mole bleeding.

No entries for the next five weeks and then:

- 18 February: 2.20 appointment re left flank—minor surgery to remove the mole!
- Later that day: "Minor surgery" took much longer than expected. A lot of bleeding. Doctor alarmed!
- 28 February: Called into Dr J's surgery. Presented with some facts and a letter from Diagnostic Med Lab.

No details were recorded, but I remember that day vividly. He phoned me with the bombshell—the "old-age spot" was a malignant melanoma. I left work and headed home with a cold feeling of fear filling every part of me. Brian met me at Constellation bus station—parked in his usual place but not looking his usual smiling self. We just held each other— knowing, yet not really knowing or believing that this could be happening to us, again.

Back to the diary:

- 2 March: Telephone conversation with Dr J— arranging a hospital appointment with a melanoma expert ASAP.

- 5 March: Saw Dr J again to check the wound—hospital appointment for 7 March, 8.45 a.m.
- 7 March: Saw specialist, Dr C, North Shore Hospital.
- 15 March: Surgery booked for 27 March
- 23 March: CT scan at Waitakere to check for spread. Petrol $1.52

## Surgery

Oncology specialist, Dr C (call me Shas!) was a delightful lady, a committed Christian who assured Brian and me that she prayed for her patients. We felt that God had led us to the right person.

Shas also called a spade a spade. Chemotherapy was not an option for melanoma; surgeries and radiation were the only treatment. Brian, as has always been his way, witnessed that he was trusting God for his healing and was grateful to know that he was in the hands of a Christian, praying doctor. He had never reached for painkillers but had spent his entire life trusting *only* in the Lord Jesus to heal him.

When 27 March arrived, the day dawned sunny and bright, not a cloud in the sky. We were shown into a small room in the day surgery unit to wait and were able to pray together, asking the Lord for the peace that passes all understanding—and for skill for the surgeon and team. I can't recall if we prayed for complete healing at that time. That was certainly our overwhelming desire, and God knew that; we both knew enough about melanoma to know that, no matter how skilled the surgeon, a miracle was needed.

When I returned to the hospital, Brian was still in the recovery ward—very groggy. The operation had taken much longer than expected, and, instead of heading home that night, he would be in hospital for five days. I went back to work Wednesday for the rest of the week—no work, no pay for contractors. Hospital visiting times needed to be juggled with work to bring in the necessary finance. Ann did daytime visiting, and I spent the evenings at the hospital. Brian was discharged on Saturday with a drain in place and recuperated at home with district nurses calling daily.

On 11 April, Dr C was upfront. "Brian this is not what you want to hear, and I don't want to be telling it to you, but it is the truth, and we need to face it." She told us melanoma was easy to identify during surgery as it was black, and there were *lots* of black spots

I don't believe he faced the truth at that point. Nor did I. Maybe it was because we were praying for a miracle of complete healing. Would it show our lack of faith to accept impending death?

## Trying to Get Back to Normal?

Brian returned to work at the Institute of Technology, focussed on preparing his group of builders for examination and assessment in July. We focussed on the cottage and family events, trying to get life back to normal. In mid-August, Brian was intent on being at Jono's eleventh birthday party at the stock cars in Silverdale, despite recovering from more surgery. Did he know this would be his last grandchild's birthday party?

Another memorable event was Jess Blackwell's baptism. When we were invited to the service, my first thought was that travelling to Mangawhai for the service and spending a day with our friends would be too much for Brian. But he was adamant we should be there—almost like stand in grandparents. The service was uplifting, and seeing Jess make her commitment and enter the water was very moving.

We were both focussed and in control until we sang the closing hymn, "I See the King of Glory". The tears started when we sang:

> Heal my heart and make it clean,
> Open up my eyes to the things unseen,
> Show me how to love like you have loved me.
> Break my heart for what breaks yours,
> Everything I am for your Kingdom's cause,
> As I walk from earth into Eternity!"

That final line said it all.

We both knew that, despite the ongoing treatment and care from the cancer unit, Brian would soon be walking from earth into eternity.

During radiation treatment in October, Brian suffered a collapse –he needed a blood transfusion. He was admitted to hospital, and one of the nurses took me aside and told me it was time I stopped working to care for my husband, telling me straight! I wish someone had told me straight earlier.

## Preparing to Head for Home

We came home on Friday, 19 October, from hospital and examined all the documents, trying to take in the medical assessments. The melanoma had spread to his liver and lungs. Brian told me firmly and plainly, "I am going".

I was still focussed on being positive, anticipating that miracle of complete healing, in denial. Kerry and Rae brought a complete cooked meal to share with us that night. Brian sat at the table, enjoying the caring company of our friends.

Next morning, I needed to do grocery shopping, and Brian opted to come with me. He sat in the Browns Bay Library reading newspapers, determined to keep going, to fill every day. He set the alarm to watch the Rugby World Cup final between France and the Springboks, on TV at an unearthly hour! Craig was watching it live in France. He and his colleagues had travelled to Europe, expecting to watch the All Blacks in the final. Springboks was a good second best for Craig.

On Sunday, 21 October, the minister from St Michael's brought Communion for Brian and me, a lovely time of prayer.

Was he administering Last Rites?

Craig broke his journey home from France in Auckland, eager to see his dad. They spent hours talking, one on one, and we shared lovely family meals with Ann, Nick, and the children. On Wednesday morning, he flew to Hawkes Bay, promising to return with Karen and Ben on Friday. Brian stayed in bed after Craig had left. He slept a lot.

Two hospice nurses came on Friday to assess Brian, their first visit. They fitted a stent to help with pain control, delivered a commode, and arranged for a high hospital bed to be delivered on Monday to help me care for Brian at home. I was taking one day at a time, but hospital wasn't part of the plan.

## Smiles through the Pain

There were a couple of amusing incidents during that time of heartbreak. One evening, I was sitting beside the bed reading while Brian slept, when Michelle Y crept into the quiet bedroom and crouched on the floor at my side. We spoke in whispers, but Brian woke from his sleep, and his eyes fixed on Michelle, his whole face lighting into a smile! And then he looked at me and his face dropped

Michelle said, "You thought you were there, didn't you?"

Brian just chuckled and nodded. He had thought Michelle was an angel in her glistening white blouse.

Karen, Ann, and I went shopping on Saturday morning. The hospice nurses had recommended adult nappy pads to help with bed care, recommending an agency in Albany. The family were drinking tea and chatting in the lounge when we returned, Brian sleeping in bed. I decided to use this time to apply the first "nappy".

Remembering that we can still hear even though asleep, I talked through the process of lifting Brian onto the pad. I asked for his cooperation so I could continue to care for him at home, but he seemed to be pushing against me, resisting my struggles. Or was he just in a deep asleep and, therefore, a dead weight?

Pad finally in place, I rearranged the covers, kissed his cheek, and was walking across the room when something hit me on the back of my head. The nappy! He was not asleep at all, just pretending and resisting this next step with the hint of a smile.

## Last Day

Monday morning was a challenge. The hospital bed was delivered by St John but by only one elderly man—no extra muscle to help lift Brian. Michelle and Dr N came on their lunch break, and with their expertise, we were able to transfer him into the high bed and pull up the sides. Dr N noticed that Brian had mucus in his throat and prescribed something to help, an injection the hospice nurse could give on her scheduled 5 p.m. visit.

I was wishing for a nap when the doorbell rang. It was dear Aurelia, who had come to sit with Brian so I could rest. A walk around the block cleared my mind and then a rest in the spare room, tea and a chat with Aurelia. She was just leaving when the hospice nurse arrived. The high bed was approved, some tips given for care, the injection administered.

"Let's go into the lounge so we don't disturb Brian," she said. "I want you to know what to expect next."

We sat at the dining room table as I leafed through information sheets and noted contact numbers. Questions were asked and answered.

Then we heard Brian cough. The nurse looked up intently and said, "I think that is it."

We rushed to the bedroom. And sure enough, Brian was not breathing. He looked as though he was just sleeping, less tension in his face, more relaxed. He had gone home. On his own! Without me holding his hand. I imagined him saying, "No more injections for me, thank you. I am off!"

Ann and the children came running in response to my call. Ann plastered lipstick on her lips and handed it to the children. They covered Brian's face with lipstick kisses, a loving send-off! As the undertaker drove away, I was herded into Ann's car to spend that Monday night sleeping in her home.

I was in a state of limbo, allowing Nick and Ann and Craig and Karen to do much of the funeral planning. This was not the first time I have been in a season of mourning. Grief is harrowing in each situation, but this one was different. My grief was undergirded with anger. I had never accepted the diagnosis and prognosis, believing in a miracle.

My family is wonderful, especially Ann. I recognise her

responses as similar to mine when my father died—she was suppressing her own mourning to support me. The loving support from family and friends during the days immediately after Brian's death was like a big soft eiderdown, protecting me from the harsh reality. Nick and Ann and Karen and Craig took care of the funeral arrangements.

## The Reality Hits Home

Brian had often quoted the scripture from Ecclesiastes 4:9 (NIV)—"Two are better than one"—usually with his arm linked through mine. And he was right; two *are* always better than one. But the fact is, I am now *one*. I am now a widow!

Many things had been put on the back-burner as the illness progressed and Brian became weaker. My intention was to get round to them "later". I heard myself telling someone that I would do that when things were "back to normal". Even as I said those words, I knew that things would never be normal again, at least not normal as I had known it.

When I was planning to become a wife, forty-nine years ago, I'd read books on marriage and how to be a good wife. Brian and I had attended marriage classes together to prepare us both for the change of status. When I became a mother, I read books and articles on parenting, accepting advice from many sources on babies, preteens, and teens.

But there were no widow's classes! How would I manage this?

So began the season of just "me"—no longer "we"—after forty-nine years shared with Brian.

Or had the "we" changed to "God and me"?

# THIRTY

## A Time to Mend

### The New Normal

A time of emptiness and desolation kicked in after the funeral, as Craig and Karen headed home, and everyone tried to adjust to life without Brian.

Fay and Bill arrived from the United Kingdom a week after the funeral. Their trip to New Zealand and Australia had been planned early in the year before the melanoma was diagnosed. They had booked two weeks of touring and exploring New Zealand, seeing the sights and visiting Fay's uncle in Gore before heading to friends in Aussie. How could we have known what the year had in store? Fay had hoped to spend time with her Uncle Brian, but she missed him by a week!

Their presence was comforting for me, an opportunity to rehash all that had happened while showing them the places we loved. It was one foot on the road to healing.

## To Build or Not to Build?

This was a time for a big decision to be made regarding my future home. Our plan had been to build on the lower end of Ann and Nick's garden. Brian had designed a cottage, and the plans had been submitted to the Council for Building Consent. He had made a connection with one of the council agents and called in regularly to follow progress. This appeared to be nil.

A new law decreed that trainee builders must have practical monitored experience in order to qualify for master builder status. Brian planned to use our cottage for his class, giving them the required experience while reducing our building costs. That option was no longer available, as Brian was no longer at the college.

As his illness progressed, our focus had moved from the cottage to his recovery. And the game plan had fully changed with Brian's death.

Now, I would need to commission a registered builder and did not have the finance to proceed. Would the whole plan be scrapped? Our small capital from the sale of our Zimbabwe home had been reduced by $20,000 already, for surveying and resource consent applications.

Nick and Ann believed we should go ahead, use my remaining capital, and put the balance onto their mortgage. The land was not large enough to subdivided, so the minor dwelling, built on their property, would be in their name anyway. Nick sourced and compared quotes from builders he knew and trusted; we agreed to go ahead with the build. The chosen builder had a free time slot; we were A for away!

But resource consent had still not been granted. I telephoned the council office and spoke to Bill, the man Brian had been dealing with:

"Hello, Bill. I am Brian Bishop's wife."

"Hi there," he replied cheerily. "I haven't seen Brian for quite a while. How's the building going?"

"Not even started yet," I replied. "No consent received."

"What?" he exclaimed. "Why hasn't Brian called me?"

"Because he was battling melanoma and died in October."

Stunned silence. "I am so very sorry to hear that," Bill said, genuine sadness in his voice. "So sorry for your loss. Brian was a great guy. I enjoyed our chats. Please give me your number. I will chase this up."

## New Home Growing

And he did, bless him! Consent was received a week later. The first sod was turned in June 2008. There was a delay while the remaining lilly-pilly tree in the garden was examined to be classified, either as a noxious weed or protected species. A team of three experts examined the tree. They could not agree—returned three different verdicts, with three bills! The truth was, whatever the experts' decision, the tree was staying. There was a swing hanging from a branch, and Grandpa had built a crude treehouse.

Building progress was steady, and the framework rapidly came together. Before the interior gibbing was applied, I wanted to write scriptures over the doors and windows. When Jonathan and Meghan saw what I was doing, they were very excited.

"Can we write some too, Nana?" they asked.

That was even better!

We agreed to have our favourite scriptures by the following evening and "bless the house" together.

When I arrived after work that Friday evening, the whole

family were eagerly waiting, pens in hand. Bethany had just started school and wanted to be part of this. She could do Jesus pictures and add a few words. My initial plan of a scripture over the door frames expanded to every frame being covered with God's word! I was amazed at how much scripture these children knew.

What would the builders think when they started work on Monday morning? They were all Christian men, so I hoped they would be as blessed and inspired as I was. And I knew I would be at peace sitting in my home surrounded by God's promises!

## New Home

The moving in date had been set for 16 December. But as the time grew closer, it was obvious there were two choices—(a) move into an unfinished house or (b) wait until after the Christmas builders' break. Our builders were committed to a ministry trip building houses in the Solomon Islands during their break, so it was 16 December or end of January. I could not wait to be in my new home so went for plan (a)—the unfinished areas would be worked around until February.

The house interior had been completed and looked attractive and welcoming. Areas of concern were lack of railings around the decks and no steps leading up to the front door. The builders had improvised access for the tradies on the garden side by making steps out of rocks leading up to the deck. These would suffice until the wooden ones were installed.

As moving day approached, my plan to call a removal company was vetoed by my Shore Grace Church family. They had stood beside Brian and me during his illness and now planned to move me into my new home! Kerry booked a drive-yourself van and brought a team of strong guys to load up my home. Raewyn gathered a group of ladies to clean up the rental, leaving me free to position the furniture in the new house.

I was awake at dawn, dressed and on a mission. No burial site had yet been chosen for Brian's ashes; they were still in my cupboard! I drove to the cottage. I lovingly carried Brian over the threshold, remembering the times he had carried me over the threshold into our various homes.

Carrying furniture up the side of the hill and using the rock steps was a challenge, even for strong men. But there were a crowd of helpers, and the job was done in record time and the van returned. Ann organised a BBQ under the lilly-pilly tree. The whole day was an exercise in love and family support. Ps Mike prayed before they left, blessing and dedicating the house to the Lord—and I felt truly blessed. All the building was completed by end of February, including the driveway and wooden fencing.

## House of Prayer

The garage space below, designed for two cars and Brian's workshop, was now underutilised. There was only one car now and no workshop. Initially, it was filled with boxes and unwanted furniture; I prayed for wisdom on how to use the area.

First on the agenda was a house-warming party, which became a house-warming party with a difference! Passover and Easter coincided that year, so the party became a Passover meal, using the Messianic Seder booklet we'd bought in Israel and used in Zimbabwe. The garage space was large enough to invite *everyone*—family, church family, and friends. Walls were decorated with posters, trestle tables borrowed and laid out in U formation, and music recorded.

People gathered on the evening of Wednesday, 8 April 2009, and Jonathan blew the shofar at sundown. Todd agreed to read the Seder, Brian's part. The meal and the singing and the re-enacting of God rescuing His people stretched out until after ten o'clock. It was a wonderful way to bless the space. My dear friend Jan told me to leave all the dishes and she would take care of them tomorrow, while I was at work.

And later in the year, that little house became the venue for Shore Grace's season of 24/7 prayer. People registered their time slot and could pray at home *or* use the prayer room in my house! The garage space was furnished with couches, chairs, and lamps on tables, giving a welcoming appeal. The side door was left unlocked so people could come and go throughout the days and nights. I could hear the occasional car as I lay in bed and some singing, especially when the youth had their hour on Friday night! And my grandchildren were drawn there after school just to sit quietly in a space filled with people's prayers, adding their own.

## Making Memories

That little house was also the backdrop for two very special memories. Nick's gran asked me to perm her hair using the home perm kit bought when she was in the United Kingdom. I had done this for her on other occasions, and we usually enjoyed the time of chatting over the lengthy, smelly process.

That Saturday afternoon, Mary was agitated and annoyed. "Where does Ann get these new-fangled ideas?" she demanded.

"What ideas?" I asked innocently, although Ann had warned me I could be in for some questioning.

"This born-again stuff!" Mary almost spat out. "Everyone has to be born again to go to heaven! Where does she get that idea from?"

Uh-oh. Ann really had given it to Mary from the hip.

I wiped my hands and grabbed my Bible. "This is not something new, Mary," I said. "Jesus laid it out very clearly. It's here in John's gospel."

I turned to John 3:3 (NIV), where Jesus said to Nicodemus, who had the same reservations as Mary, "I tell you the truth, no one can see the kingdom of God unless he is born again."

A look of surprise spread over Mary's face. "I must have read that but don't remember the born-again bit." She sat still, thoughtful as I continued reading verse five.

"It's not difficult, Mary. We can say a prayer together right now if you'd like, asking Jesus to be Lord of your life."

She smiled, patted my hand, and said, "It's all right, lovie."

I mopped up the perm lotion drips, put another cloth around her neck, and set the timer, wondering what next.

"Tea or coffee, Mary?"

"A cup of tea would be nice," she answered with a smile.

I headed for the kitchen and returned ten minutes later, mugs in hand, to find Mary sitting, head bowed, hands together, eyes closed in prayer. Holding my breath, I backed out, leaving her to ask Jesus to be her Lord and Saviour in her own words. Born again at 95!

The other special memory came a couple of years later, on a rare night that I'd managed to get to bed early with tea and a good book. I heard voices coming down the path from the main house, serious discussion going on in hushed tones. I looked at the clock. It was after ten—what could have happened?

I leapt out of bed and unlocked the lounge door to let the whole family file in with sombre looks on their faces.

251

Meghan spoke first. "Nana, how many grandchildren do you have?"

"Four!" *Oh no. Has something happened to Ben?* The other three were standing in front of me!

"No, you don't," said Meg, still looking serious. "You have *five*!"

They all burst into laughter at once—probably looking at my open mouth.

I turned to Ann. "What? Are you pregnant?"

She nodded, and the hugs and tears started then.

Nick and Ann had come to terms with this shocking discovery, not on the agenda in the middle of Ann's studying for a counselling degree. They had taken the three children, aged eight, twelve, and fifteen, out for dessert to make the announcement. Seeing my bedroom light still on when they returned, I was the next target to be surprised.

Isaac Brian Simcoe Read arrived six months later—bringing so much joy into all our lives.

# THIRTY-ONE

# A Time to Throw Away
# ... Bad Attitudes

## What Season is This Lord?

The year of the cottage build had started on such a high note but ended with a time of great turmoil and rejection in my life, such as I had never experienced. It was a time when I felt belittled, beaten down, and very alone. No Brian to share my feelings with or hold me close. I tried to lean on God, calling out to Him, praying from my heart, and writing those prayers in my journal.

Rereading those notes now, I can see it as a time when God was teaching me to trust Him in difficult situations:

–   29 December 2009 (post-Christmas)
    The past two weeks have been very hard. My contract was extended yet again until the end of March 2010, providing income, but now I'm having second thoughts. Mel has left and the Recoveries Department is just me! I am on

my own, swamped, and sinking beneath the volume of work, which has escalated beyond any hope of clearing it single-handedly. Each day, there are more businesses in receivership or liquidation—each notification requiring hours of work. The inbox was full when I left the office on Christmas Eve.

The pressure and stress of handling the workload single-handedly is only one side of the coin. The real heartache has been the new management team of N and E and their plan to recruit new staff, which does not include me. I am to be jettisoned!

Please help, Lord. I know I have lessons to learn, but what is this lesson?.

– 30 December 2009 (time to take stock)
Lord, I am mulling over all that has happened, trying to decide what to do. Please guide me as I record events and try to sort out what has happened.

My initial six-month contract has been renewed every three months over four years. I assumed that, when a permanent post was available, I would be offered it. Who was it who said, "Never assume"? Previous managers bent the law to keep me, but now I am to be discarded, replaced! New manager N advised me to, "Look after your own interests and see what other work is out there."

He also said I was not considered suitable for either of the positions—even though I have been doing the work for eighteen months, single-handedly, complimented and encouraged by other managers.

No suitable applicants were found from within the company, so I was given an interview date, raising my hopes. The interview with the new manager and Lara from HR stretched over two hours. The questions were not the usual interview questions and when the word insubordination was used, I realised that this was, in fact, a disciplinary meeting. Have I been insubordinate?

When I was advised by email, on Christmas Eve, that the job had been given to someone else, reason given was, my "resistance to change". A second email assured me that, "Management will understand that your numbers will be down during the time you will be training the new credit controller."

What? Surely not!

## Plan of Action

The new credit controller was due to start in February. So, it appeared my contract had been extended by two months for the sole purpose of allowing me time to train her. The compulsory Christmas / New Year break for contractors gave me ten days to consider my next step.

Writing these events in my journal and praying over them helped formulate a plan of action. I would not accept the two-month extension but, rather, would leave the company on 29 January 2010 when my current contract ended. *Father, please give me the wisdom to know if this is the right course of action or direct events, please, Lord, so I know what your purpose is for my life.*

I returned to work on 4 January but. Before I could hand in my notice, I received an email from manager N: "I would like you to apply for the next role when it is advertised.

What was happening? A change of heart?

My next journal entry was 10 January 2010:

> This morning, we sang of the refiner's fire.
>
> "Purify my heart, make me as pure gold"
>
> I sang with gusto until I realised what I was asking!
>
> Am I in the refiner's fire?
>
> The message this morning was from Matthew 5:38–47, instruction to God's people about retaliation and loving our Enemies!
>
> Lord, help! I can't do that on my own; it needs to be your love, Jesus.

I started to pray intentionally for N in his position as new manager, something I should have been doing from day one. Throughout January 2010 I battled on single-handedly, but the climate had changed. My contract was extended for another two months, undisputed by me. Was God working in both of us?

P joined me at the beginning of February in Recoveries, and although I did not officially train her, we became firm friends and shared our knowledge and expertise. I discovered she had been assured of the credit control position in November, before my first gruelling interview. Our company had bought out another smaller Telco and guaranteed employment to selected staff.

## Another Chance

The second credit controller role was advertised, and I knew that, when this position was filled, my contract would finally end. An interview as offered to me by HR, and I determined to go well armed! The previous interview had given me insight into the type of questions I could expect, and I prepared responses, gathering examples from my past working career and current customers.

Once again, Lara and N were the interviewers—Lara in the driving seat this time. With every response I made to her questions, she expressed her approval, praise, and appreciation, deferring to N to allow him to also give his approval. This was not easy for him if he still had hopes of replacing this experienced old lady with a bright young person.

The interview ended around 4.15 p.m., and I went home shortly after, feeling I had given it my best shot. The result was God's business!

My desk phone shrilled as I arrived next morning.

"You've got the job!" Lara shrieked in my ear. "I wanted to call you last night but didn't have your mobile number." She said the two other applicants could not touch me. I had run rings around them.

All eyes in the collections team were on me as they listened to my side of the conversation. I gave them the thumbs up, and they raised a loud cheer. N raised his eyebrows! At last, I had a permanent position.

Was that gruelling season all about *changing me*? And if so, what had changed?

## What Have I Learned?

I learned to *trust God*—in all circumstances. I needed to work to eat; my Zimbabwe pension was non-remittable, and I was not eligible for Kiwi superannuation.

I learned how to *hand over* the whole situation to *God* and not keep taking it back—to believe He was in the driving seat even when the wheels were off and to know peace whatever outcome.

I learned to *ask* my Abba daily for whatever I needed—wisdom, strength, stamina, sleep.

I learned that there was *conflict* in Jesus's day, and He gave clear instructions in His instruction manual how to deal with it:

> *Settle* disputes before you get to court. (Matthew 5: 25)
> *Forgive* as God forgives me. (Matthew 6:14 and 18:21–22)
> *Love* your neighbour as yourself. (Mark 12:31)
> *Turn* the other cheek. (Matthew 5:39)
> *Go* the extra mile. (Matthew 5:41)
> *Love* your enemies, (Matthew 5:44)
> *Pray* for those who despitefully use you. (Matthew 5:44)

Matthew 5:44 (NIV) was the game changer. "But I say unto you, love your enemies, bless them that curse you, do good to them that hate you, and pray for them which despitefully use you, and persecute you." When I started praying for N the man instead of my situation, there was a paradigm shift! We had some meaningful discussions. I saw him as a young husband and father, wanting to be the best provider for his family. Meeting his lovely wife Kay helped complete the picture.

Subsequent restructures increased the team to four, spreading the workload, with a new manager, S. This was the third restructure in the company since 2010—another lesson learned: Nothing stays the same forever in this fallen world.

# THIRTY-TWO

# A Time to Tear Down and a Time to Rebuild

## Retirement

Five years later, I entered that mystical season of retirement!

My emotions were in turmoil when I left the company after ten years. The routine of my life was about to change radically. No more rushing for a place in the car park before 7 a.m. No more cramming the rest of life into evenings and weekends. But no more days spent with colleagues who had become friends, sharing lunch dates and events.

As I read the messages on my cards, I had a deep sense of loss—and of failure. For ten years, I had worked alongside a mix of people of all ages and stages—from open-minded Hindus to devout Muslim to nominal Christian believers to confessing atheists. They had all written such kind encouraging words, telling me how much I would be missed, extolling my wisdom, spelling, and grammar expertise, and even my singing, but there was no reference on those cards of any spiritual connection.

There had been meaningful discussion and prayer in times of need, and I had prayed for my colleagues to come to know Jesus as their Lord. But there was no evidence of change when I waved goodbye on 31 March! Had I failed? That was my feeling as I exited the building. Did I just need to be content to be the seed sower and leave the harvesting to others as Jesus described in John 4:3. I resolved not to "retire" from praying for my former colleagues.

## "Re*fire*ment"

Does retirement really exist? Is it a time to tear down the old patterns or a time to rebuild new ones? Or both. I can find only one mention of retirement in the Bible, and that relates to the priests! Is it God's will for His children? Moses worked to the end of his life, accepting, reluctantly, a new challenge at 80 and leading the children of Israel until he was 120 years old!

Should the season be renamed re*fire*ment—still fired up and with time to do the important stuff? The stuff we put on the back-burner during our working years?

Numerous ads on TV show the wonderful life offered to those living in retirement villages—images of beaming seniors playing games in lovely surroundings. Was this all that was left? Playing games and being entertained until clogs are popped? I saw myself as a "doer", and the idea of endless days of fun and socialising, without anything productive to show at the end of the day, held no appeal for me. I dragged my feet, reluctant to face the challenge of my working life coming to an end, a feeling of being "put out to pasture"!

My journal records my thoughts on getting **older** (15 July 2009): Life begins at 70! Oh yeah! Three score and ten!" A lengthy prayer followed.

261

The joy of being a journaler is reading past prayers and discovering how they have been answered! I had survived the trauma of Brian's illness and death, adjusted to life on my own, built the cottage that had been our joint dream, and moved in without him. I had prayed for and pursued permanent employment status, which had been granted by the management team who initially wanted to eject me. The company had no official date for retirement, and I welcomed the opportunity to be productive, learning new skills at an age when many people were reduced to watching daytime TV.

In July 2014, when I turned 75, I started to think seriously about retirement. I prayed about it, really wanting a specific instruction from God telling me, "*Now* is the right time to retire."

I know He is my provider, and I'd qualified for superannuation, so I wasn't destitute. But I no longer owned my home. Nor did I have a large nest egg. I had only a small amount invested on term deposit and some current accessible savings for trips, car repairs, and anything big! I could only see a steady dwindling of the balance and a tightening of belts as my financial reserves diminished, not replenished without full-time work—not exactly faith-filled thoughts! Had I forgotten that I was a King's kid!? I made budgets and continued to drag my heels, still praying for that writing in the sky.

A journal note recorded on 15 July 2015, upon turning 76, reads, "My Loving Heavenly Father; I feel the need to speak to son-in-law Nick about timing of retirement—please bless this discussion."

Next note: "Nick agreed that the end of the year would be good, as Ann will have finished her studies and be ready to start her new career."

No more journal entries about retirement until Sunday, 26 October 2015:

"Attended Millwater Church for the morning service instead of Shore Grace. Pastor John asked the congregation to share what God had been doing in their lives since last Sunday or any Word they had received. I was praying during the silence, once again, for God to direct my paths and show me when I should retire and what was the next step.

Then Pauline walked to the front of the church and said, "I really don't know what this means or who it is for, but God says, 'It is time.'"

## Planning

Was my Heavenly Father rolling His eyes? I knew that word was for me, and I needed to be obedient. So, I claimed it! Now it was time for action. A few more days of mulling it over, and I gave notice to leave at the end of January 2016. Amy was due back from maternity leave in February, so I would not be leaving the team in the lurch. Deed done—finally.

The note in my journal that day records my fears. These were linked to my finances or lack of. Could I live on the super? I had previously recorded in my journal a list of loose ends to be tied up while still earning. Now I added, "Find work elsewhere two or three days a week."

The Word for Today quotes Psalms 127:1 (NIV): "Unless the Lord builds the house its builders labour in vain!" My journal note reads, "I don't want to go ahead of you, Lord. I will wait on You and trust You as my Lord and my Provider."

The following Sunday after church, Michelle asked how my week had gone. When I told her I'd finally given notice to retire at the end of January, her response was a joyful, "Yahoo." Michelle and Amanda had been praying for the right person to take on the Community Trust role of Neighbourhood Support facilitator. They had me in mind, but I was still clinging to my full-time job. God had answered *all* our prayers!

The trust vacancy was from the end of December, but the committee agreed I could start in February when my full-time work finished. That was perfect. But the timetable changed again when my manager, S asked if I could stay on until the financial year end, 31 March 2016. We negotiated two days with the company and two days with the trust from February. It made for a smooth transition from full-time commercial employment to community work, with added income and a purpose to my life. Win-win!

My God supplies all my needs, according to His riches in glory!

# THIRTY-THREE

# A Time to Live Till I Die

## Celebrating Fourscore

Milestones seem to come around quicker as the years tick by! Another party was planned for my eightieth. A sort of ceilidh with a fifties theme—circular skirts, frilly petticoats, ponytails, bright red lipstick, braces, and rolled up pants for the guys and dancing to rock and roll music. Sixty-three friends turned out on a very cold night to celebrate with me, warmed by mulled wine, fun, and laughter. Meg had compiled songbooks for a singalong, intended as a rest time between dances, but the dance party started again when the song was "I Saw her Standing There". Everyone on the dance floor was rocking and rolling again, just like in the fifties. Even those who said they couldn't dance, wouldn't dance, were dancing!

The blessings, lunches, dinners, and special teas extended over the next two weeks. I received cards with loving words from wonderful family and friends and many beautiful, thoughtful gifts, each one showing the giver's love.

One piece of jewellery is a constant reminder on my hand of God's blessing and His goodness to me. An exquisite gold ring set with a variety of precious stones, eleven in all, each a different colour and size, some very tiny, others claiming prominence, making a combined statement of beauty. Ann explained that they represented all the children God had given me—my two children, Craig and Ann; my three foster children, Fay, Gail, and Katie; my five grandchildren, Ben, Jono, Meg, Beth, and Isaac; and James, the precious little baby I had miscarried. And I was once a barren woman!

## Live until I Die

My prayer is to *live* until I *die*—to grow intellectually and spiritually and to do new and meaningful things. I love pottering in the garden or watching a good TV program for relaxation, but I would hate this to be my entire life, just filling each day, marking time until the final whistle blows. I want to be useful right up until time to go time, not just exist or potter about, not become *old*!

I don't mind the numbers clocking up as I add to my bucket list. I just don't want to *be* old. That song from the fifties captures my sentiments in a nutshell:

> I'm gonna live till I die! I'm gonna shout
> *yipee aye*!
> I'm gonna take this town and turn it upside
> down
> I'm gonna live, live, live until I die!

Leaving this aging "tent" behind holds no fear for me, but I just don't want to *be old*. I still feel like I'm 33 on the inside; the reflection in the mirror is a shock, a reality call. That new body will be a great gift. Meanwhile, I slap on the face cream and focus on the instruction in Romans 12:2 (NIV), "Be transformed by the renewing of your minds."

## Coping with Retirement

So, what has triggered these thoughts. I am, in fact, only semi-retired; I have a facilitator's job for ten hours weekly. Add in some volunteering, and those ten hours weekly have morphed into a 24/7 new way of approaching each day. My eyes have been opened to issues I was unaware of when working in the "young" environment of telecommunications.

Tuesday morning sees a group assembling at the community house. All are retirees, over 65, mostly immigrants. Some have immigrated from China to live with their only child, becoming lonely when their families are at work and isolated by the language barrier. Sharing tea and biscuits with others in similar circumstances puts smiles on faces and gives a feeling of community.

A Mandarin-speaking teacher was hired to teach English, but class numbers dwindled as Covid took over our lives. Learning English is a priority for this group, so we needed new initiatives—fun ways to learn the language. So, line dancing using English words for dance moves, singalongs to English songs, and word games became the new way to learn English.

Recently, I volunteered at the secure care unit of a local retirement village.

This is where those seniors who are unable to manage their lives independently are given around-the-clock care. There are about thirty-five people in this wing, some over 90 years old, others younger than I am. Some are well supported by family and friends; others rarely have visitors. The staff are kind and caring, showing love even to those who are hard to love. They are imaginative and constructive in their efforts to help each person enjoy every day.

I arrive after morning tea has been served and chair exercises are under way in the lounge. Then it's time for knitting. The numbers vary. Some refuse outright. Some agree reluctantly. Only a few accept the needles and wool with an attitude that says, "Oh great, it's knitting time!"

That's when I hear the word *can't* a lot. "I can't knit anymore." "Can't hold the needles—my hands shake too much." "I can't see very well." "Can't stay. Going home soon!"

Some sit and chat. Others just nod off or sit silent with their own thoughts, watching the clock until lunch.

My prayer: *Father, how does this confusion happen?* This is not how I want to end my days!

## Fear or Faith-Based Thoughts

A leading neurosurgeon was the keynote speaker at a Christian women's conference I attended a few years back. She stated that 87 per cent of all illnesses start in our heads, as thoughts, either fear-based or faith-based, which affect emotions, attitude, and behaviour. An EEG-type scan showed how negative thoughts make a black hole in our brain connectivity. The good news was that these black holes can be reversed, when negative thoughts are taken captive and turned into positive thoughts! Dr L confirmed the physical facts with scriptural promises.

That conference gave me assurance that losing my marbles is not God's will for me! Everything needed is in the manufacturer's handbook—the Bible. I just need to read it and believe God's word.

## What *Does* the Bible Have to Say?

God's word gives guidance for every aspect of our lives.

- *Sound mind.* "For God has not given us a spirit of fear but of power, and of love and of a sound mind" (2 Timothy 1:7, NLJV). I need to recognise fear-based thoughts, reject them, and replace them with God's promises.

- *Wisdom.* This age of information overload can be challenging, and my memory does fail, especially when I'm overtired. But God's word gives hope and direction in James 1:5 (NIV): "If anyone of you lacks wisdom, he should ask God, who gives generously to all. . God gives wisdom to *all* who ask; I just need to ask!

- *Healing.* Isaiah 53:5 (NIV) tells us, "And by His wounds we *are* healed." The healing is already done by Jesus; it's not "going to be done one day". Jesus received thirty-nine lashes on his back. He took them for me—for all of us! I need to declare the truth to the enemy and affirm the healing and give thanks to God.

- *Strength and stamina.* "The Joy of the Lord is my strength." How often do I focus on feeling "tired/ exhausted" and give this as the reason, or excuse, for inactivity? Even speaking the words "I am tired" is draining, *but* when I declare God's promise in Nehemiah 8:10 (NIV) "The Joy of the Lord is my Strength" or David's in Psalm 28: 7 (NIV) "The Lord is my strength and shield", my strength is renewed. Moses declared in Exodus 15 that God renewed his strength, at age 80, to lead the children of Israel out of Egypt—meandering through the wilderness for forty years until he was 120! No retirement for Moses.

- *Authority.* Jesus gave His followers, His disciples, and believers like you and me the authority to "place their hands on sick people and they will get well" (Mark 16:18, NIV). How often do I ask Jesus to do the healing instead of taking up the authority He gave me and laying hands on the sick in His name? Is this "passing the buck?

  *Ability.* When God calls us to do something we feel not qualified to do, He equips us. 1Thess 5: 24 (NIV) states, "He who calls you is faithful and he will do it." And Ephesians 3:20 (NIV) tells us, "Now to him who is able to do immeasurably more than all we ask or imagine, according to the power at work within us."

- So, my resolve is to cut back on the "I can'ts", give new things a try, and trust that the Lord will empower me. I accept they may take longer to achieve at 82 than they would at 28!

Whatever the challenge, like the song says, I wanna *live* till I die—not just exist. I want to celebrate every day as a gift from God.